John Schneider

MY LIFE, MY WAY

WITH JAMIE BLAINE & RIVER JORDAN

MY LIFE, MY WAY

First Edition

Cover design by Angela Blake

10   9   8   7   6   5   4   3   2   1

Printed in the United States of America.

DISCLAIMER

We changed some things. Names, places, faces. To protect the innocent, the guilty, those who simply didn't know any better at the time. The stories are loosely chronological and told to the best of my recollection. Certain scenes have been edited and compressed for the sake of clarity. Everything here is true, but it's my truth – and personal truth is more like a river than a stone. It's always moving and changing and rolling on. This is my book, my life, my story. So, I'm doing it the only way I know how – my way.

While we're at it: Kids, don't try this at home. Card subject to change. Contents may settle during shipping. Any resemblance to persons living or dead, is purely coincidental. Do not use while operating a motor vehicle. Not responsible for direct, indirect, incidental, or consequential damages resulting from any defect, error, or failure to perform. The following contains adult language, brief nudity, violence, crude humor, and mature themes. Discretion is advised. Deal with it.

Also, when I say "we," I mean that it takes a team to create a book. Two Nashville writers helped gather my thoughts and arrange them on the page. Jamie Blaine on *The Dukes of Hazzard* and music. On childhood, Cash, and post-Dukes projects, River Jordan.

Now that we've got that out of the way, hang on. We're goin' for a ride!

THE JUMP: SOMETHING IN THE DISTANCE (I AM BO DUKE)

*"Courage is being scared to death but
saddling up anyway." – John Wayne*

April 6, 2019

The black helicopter carries me over the trees as I survey the scene below. Ferris wheels, food vendors, and port-a-johns are scattered across a muddy field. A launch ramp sits at the end of a long dirt road, and the crowd stretches nearly as far as I can see. Next to the ramp, one bright orange car with a rebel flag on top and a black 01 painted on both doors. Welcome to my back yard, John Schneider Studios, the place I now call home.

The pilot circles and hovers over the car. I grip the frame and step out onto the landing skid as we start a slow descent.

"Get away from the 'copter quick as you can, John," the pilot shouts. "We wouldn't want the tail rotor to catch you coming up."

"Will do," I say, thumbs-up in agreement.

"One more thing," adds stunt coordinator Jack Gill. "When you wave to the crowd, wave out, not up. Wave up and you'll lose both hands to the elbow."

"Uh, got it," I reply. The devil is always in the details, it seems.

The pilot descends, and I wave out – not up – as he gracefully sets one skid on the roof of the General Lee. I hop out onto the world's most famous car and away from the spinning blades as the helicopter lifts and vanishes back over the trees. Arms raised, I stand on the X of stars and salute the crowd.

Thank God, it's not raining, I think, as I slide through the window into the driver's seat.

The weatherman said that storms were certain, but it's seventy-nine degrees and sunshine at the second annual Bo's Extravaganza in the backwoods of South Louisiana. Rain could've ruined everything. Rain killed attendance and cancelled last year's jump. Rainwater flooded my home and studio not once, but twice. What the rain didn't ruin, I had to sell. My original General Lee. All my memorabilia, piece by piece. The headlines said, *Bo Duke is broke* while gossip sites crowed, *Bo faces jail.*

I've made nearly two hundred movies and TV shows, playing hero, crook, preacher, devil, and everything in between, starring in projects from cartoons to video games. My bio says filmmaker, director, chart-topping musician, celebrity dancer, co-founder of one of America's biggest charities, and current star of Tyler Perry's top-rated cable hit, *The Haves and the Have Nots.* But to most of the world, I am still Bo Duke, your favorite redneck cousin next door.

So here I am at the wheel of an old Crown Victoria that we rebuilt to look like the General. In the back yard of my rebuilt home. Rebuilding my life again. And for the first time ever, a Duke boy is going to jump the General Lee.

There's a lot riding on this moment. I look out over the faces and find Alicia. Soulmate, business partner, love of my life. She's walked with me through the best and worst of times. Whatever twisted road I was on brought me her way, and for that, thank God. But I hate being the reason for that worried look in her eyes. "You good, boss?" Trent asks. My right-hand man is close by, as always. Everybody needs someone like these two. People who've watched you lose it all and still stand by your side.

That's when a second thought enters my mind. *Oh, shit, it's not raining. Everybody's here. I really have to jump this car.*

The V8 roars as I give it hell. I tear through the field and cut the wheel hard, tires slinging mud to a chorus of *YEE-HAAs!* After a few more 180s, I motor up the road and prepare for takeoff. Helmet, check. Gauges look good. Five-point harness fastened and secure.

The exhaust rumbles like a dragon in heat, and the crowd is hushed, cellphones lifted to capture my fate. I punch it and speed toward the ramp. Fifty yards. Thirty-five. Twenty...

Stunt coordinator Jack Gill waves me off. I hit the brakes and skid to a dusty stop. Jack leans into my window for last-minute words of advice. "Just aim for that big sweet gum tree on the other side of the field," he tells me.

Jack Gill was one of our original stunt drivers back on Dukes and more recently, *The Fast and Furious* franchise. I've got total faith in his skills. He built the ramp, formulated my speed and angle. "Do what now?" I ask.

"You won't be able to see the landing," Jack explains, mimicking the arc of the car with his hand. "So, if you wanna make it over, you gotta aim for something in the distance."

I nod back. Tension mounts in the field as we rehearse the details once more. Finally, Jack winks and gives my shoulder a slap. "Can't just gun it and go, can we?" he says with a grin. "Gotta give the people a show."

"In that case, let's do it again. Wave me off last second, and I'll skid halfway up the ramp. Then run over shaking a finger at me like you're mad as hell."

"Got it," says Jack.

We tease out the drama, and the audience eats it up. Hey, show business.

I reset for a third run, this time driving to the top of the ramp so everyone can see the car and that it's actually me inside driving. Then I head back up the road for one last shot.

First few runs? No problem. I've done hundreds of test runs like that back on *Dukes of Hazzard*. Runs at the ramp for the camera, a few passes to get a good look at the car. But all those times, before the big jump, I climbed out and let a stuntman take the wheel. For years, kids have asked, "What's it like to jump the General Lee?" It always bothered me that I couldn't answer that question. Somehow, I felt like a fake.

So today, there is no switch, no stuntman. Just me and Bo's General Lee.

I sit revving the horses and staring toward the ramp that will launch thirty-eight hundred pounds of flesh and steel into the air, over a Livingston Parish patrol car, and with any luck –back down to a pile of hay and stacked tires to cushion the impact of my fall. Nearly nine thousand fans are packed on the sidelines, with countless more watching online, from all across the planet.

Scared? Hell, yes, I'm scared. If what you're doing doesn't scare you now and then, are you truly pursuing something worthwhile? Are you really even alive?

I've spent a lifetime behind the wheel of this car. They might as well bury me in the General Lee. *But hopefully, not today. Now or never,* I tell myself. *Don't overthink it, John.*

I hit the gas and barrel down the dirt road, a second cop car behind me, giving chase. The GPS speedometer beeps as the needle reaches forty miles per hour. Forty might seem slow, but as car jumps go, it's fast enough to half kill yourself if something goes wrong. Hundred and forty? At least at that speed, there's no pain. I am not afraid to die while doing something stupid. I'm afraid to *get hurt* doing something stupid. Chances of death in this backyard car stunt are slim, but chances of getting hurt? Pretty damn good.

Eyes on the sweet gum, I grip the wheel as we hit the ramp. The lumber groans under the weight as the crowd holds one long breath. Suddenly, I am in flight.

Time crawls when you're airborne. Back on the show, they'd freeze-frame the General in mid-air before pausing for commercial break. That's how it feels, like the whole world is on pause. I can almost hear Ol' Waylon from the other side.

Hoss, don't go to the 'frigerator now.

I think about all the people who've shown up to cheer me on. The fans, the friends, those who supported me through my most difficult time. I think about the friends and family who've crossed over to that other side. Denver, Jimmie, Sorrell, Waylon, Burt. Mom and Dad both gone now.

Making a jump in the General Lee seems symbolic of everything I've overcome in the last few years. Legal troubles, financial troubles, floods, and heartbreak, the four decades that have passed since *The Dukes of Hazzard* began. Jumping an orange muscle car for your fifty-ninth birthday. Crazy, right? Or is it?

Hang on a second. Throw it in reverse. Let's take it back to where it all began...

ACT I:
NEW YORK TO GEORGIA

*"I got vision and the rest of
the world wears bifocals."*
— Butch Cassidy and the Sundance Kid

"Not much sense in having a small dream."
— John R. Schneider

IN THE GOOD OL' DAYS

"I want to reminisce…" – John R. Schneider

In my early years growing up in upstate New York, I spent a lot of time with my Grandma Dugan and her husband, Mike. My mother was a single mom and worked, so at a young age, I mean as young as about six years old, I'd get on the bus by myself and ride from Bedford Hills to Katonah. Looking back on it now it seems like I was such a little bitty thing. I remember putting my nickels in a glass coin separator to get on the bus, and if I was ever lucky enough to have a dollar, I'd give it to the bus driver, and he actually had a change machine on his belt. I can remember the sound of it to this day. That chica, chica, chica, as he got the coins out, and he'd give my change back to me without ever looking down. I recognized skill even at a young age.

It is so odd to me to even have this memory now because with all of our fast advances in technology, with my being on my phone all the time and Facebooking with everyone and doing live FaceTime updates to our fans and followers, it seems that all of these memories are in vivid black and white. Like an episode of *The Little Rascals.* Even so I sometimes wonder how I could possibly remember taking a bus ride that cost eleven cents. But I did that. Maybe it's because of the simplicity, at least in my mind, of those times. If you look at them deeply enough, all times are simple, and all times are complicated. It all depends on your perspective at the time. Consider that for a few seconds before reading on.

I got on the bus at the corner of my house, and the bus driver would say, "Good morning, young man," pat that glass coin jar there bolted to the floor, and I'd proudly put in my change. The ride was only about fifteen minutes, but that was a long journey for a six-year-old kid, and then the bus would pull up at the corner on Grandma Dugan's street. I'd get off and walk up to her house and let myself in. She'd be inside usually cooking up something like fried Spam and eggs in a cast iron skillet. Yup… Spam. I still love me some fried Spam. Deal with it.

My grandmother was an interesting character. She was from Sanford, Florida. My mother's father, her first husband, was killed in his souped-up Model T Ford when he tried to pass a truck full of oranges on a board-straight Florida backroad. Rumor is he cut back into the lane too soon and caught his back bumper to the front bumper of the truck. Knowing now what I know about stunts and driving, I know how easy that accident is to have and to avoid. Only takes a second and it's all over. One mistake too many.

Eventually, Grandma went looking for another husband and found a couple. Her third husband, Mike Dugan, was the man I really consider my maternal grandfather. I'm glad she kept looking because he was this boy's best friend. Now, don't get the wrong idea. Grandma Dugan wasn't loose; she was just lonely, and in those days people realized that it took two incomes to run a household. Marriages were business arrangements first and romantic entanglements second. At least that's my take on it.

Sanford, Florida, is about forty miles outside of Orlando. It's a big place now, of course, but back in the sixties when my mom would put us all together to go down to see my great-grandmother and my grandmother's sister, Aunt Rene, there wasn't much around there. An air force base; a tired, old zoo; and a public swimming pool. In the early seventies we even flew a couple of times. I wish I still had the film I took out the window of the clouds and the towns that looked like the ones you see on a model railroad set up. I thought that was very cool. I also remember walking down the rolling stairs of the plane and walking right through the chain link gate where Aunt Rene was waiting with her car. Seems to me it was about thirty steps. No security, no jetway... hell, I don't even remember a terminal, although I'm sure there must have been at least a building with a ticket desk!

I called my great-grandmother Grandma Vickry. They say we have Cherokee blood in our family, and to look at Grandma Vickry you'd see it right away. She looked very Cherokee. Very much like those beautiful faces you still see in the classic John Ford Westerns. She was small and round and had kind, inquisitive eyes. They say the eyes are the window of the soul, and when I think of her, I always think about her eyes -- the kindness and peace she held in them.

Back to Grandma Dugan. She was a Green Stamp gal. She collected Green Stamps and put them in those books. I'd help her paste them in. The fatter they were, the closer you were to being able to get something special from the S&H Green-Stamp catalog.

For you folks who don't have a clue about what a Green Stamp is, a Green Stamp was magic to a kid in the sixties! Green Stamp was a rewards program for shoppers at Sperry and Hutchinson stores. Mainly, the stamps came from grocery stores, but also from some department stores and gas stations. The company used to brag they gave out three times more stamps than the U.S. Post Office, so that gives you an idea of how popular they were in the sixties. For every dollar you spent, you earned a certain number of stamps. It seemed like everybody you knew was collecting for something, and certainly kids had their eyes on the choicest toys and electronics in the catalogs — like reel to-reel-portable tape recorders.

Grandma Dugan would have me pick something out of that catalog way ahead of time, and then she and I would start collecting those sheets of stamps. Sometimes you would get a portion of a sheet or even a single stamp. A full sheet was easy to lick and put into the book, and it looked nice. Uniform. But I always liked a puzzle and actually preferred to try to make individual stamps look like a sheet. Not really possible, but everybody's got to have a hobby!

I loved seeing those books get fatter and fatter. I can still remember the taste of the glue as I helped her paste them in. It was how I got my first Bell and Howell Super-8 movie camera, the one I used to take the movies from the 707 on the way to Sanford, Florida. They used to have this big ad in the newspaper that said, "Come get this new Super 8 camera, but don't bring money." That was the big start of my movie career right there. I guess we can give a major portion of the credit to Grandma Dugan and those Green Stamps for helping me get off to an early start.

Grandpa Dugan worked about two hundred yards from their house at the Clark Funeral Home. Like I said, Grandpa Dugan was my buddy. I'd go hang with him while he worked there at the funeral home, but I'd also stay with him while he did other jobs. He was the caretaker for a bunch of cemeteries around town, and he'd also work on someone's car sometimes.

Whatever he was doing, I was just happy to be there hanging out with him. It didn't matter what specifically he was up to; I was just along for the ride.

Many years later I bought a 1947 Chevy panel truck because it reminded me of the truck he drove at the cemetery, especially the way the gears would grind when it shifted. That truck didn't have synchromesh. You had to time it perfectly for it not to sound like a meat grinder. I remember a friend of mine saying, "Hey, John... grind me a pound!" I loved that old truck because it reminded me of my grandpa.

One fun fact is that he actually had a part in a movie, *The Kremlin Letter*. It was a movie about the Cold War and starred Peter Lawford. It was something about a Naval intelligence officer who had some kind of a photographic memory, so he ends up in the CIA, and somehow that involved using caskets in this covert operation. My grandpa played a pallbearer because that was his job sometimes during the funerals. So, looking back on it, Grandpa Dugan and I had movie-making in common too.

I hung out in the funeral home all the time with Grandpa Dugan. I remember taking naps in different caskets when I was little. I mean here I was, six, seven, and eight years old, and I thought taking naps in caskets was the most normal thing in the world. It was nice and cool and had a soft silk lining, so it was pretty darn comfortable. The caskets were much more comfortable than that crappy, musty couch had been downstairs there next to the Coke machine.

Now, you might think that having a grandpa who let you hang out in the funeral home with him and follow him around through different cemeteries was about as cool as it could get, but it did get even cooler than that. He was also a volunteer firefighter with the Katonah Fire Department. Every year in June the Katonah Fire Department had a parade in the Summer that marched right down main street. It ended with their having a big carnival on the empty lot behind the fire station.

Every year I got to march in the parade with Grandpa Dugan. A few times my brother, Bob, joined us. We were dressed up as clowns, and we would put on the full clown costume and make-up in the basement of the old Kellogg and Lawrence Hardware store downtown. Hell, that was where everything was. The downtown was the lifeblood of the town back then. This was before all the malls, and strip malls, and big box stores were built.

If you needed to shop or wanted to do something, you went downtown. Once we were dressed and clowned up, we would drive up to the top of the hill where the high school was and wait for the parade to start. Bands were fun, but everybody loved "Dugan's Clowns!" Seems to me that being one of grandpa's clowns fueled my "ham" quite a bit.

I want to reminisce about that great old hardware store for a second here. Kellogg and Lawrence had already been around since 1887. I loved to just walk around and look at everything. I still can't imagine that there was anything you could possibly need that you couldn't find in that store. And it absolutely *was not* a big place. In those days it was "the customer comes first," so the shelves were put together in a friendly, easy way so that you could find anything and everything, and somehow they didn't need to be big. I loved that store. Now picture this. I'm getting to march right into that hardware store and down in the basement like I'm the mayor of the city or something and get my own clown outfit on. They sat me up on the pool table they had down there for me to have my face all made up. Then we go marching high and mighty right down the middle of Main Street behind the fire trucks. I just don't know anything a kid could enjoy more than that.

We would go walking side by side on that summer night with what looked like the whole city of Katonah turned out and lining the streets. Marching bands played, and the music filled the air. The parade ended with a big carnival set up on the empty lot behind the firehouse. When I was a kid it seemed like it was huge, about the size of Manhattan. I've been back there since and was shocked to see how small it actually is. If you want a shock, try going back to someplace you haven't been to since you were under ten. You've gotten bigger, and it's gotten smaller. Personally... I'd rather it was the size of Manhattan!

There were all these rides like Tilt-A-Whirl and the Paratrooper, and my friends from across the street and my "cousin" Jeffrey Champlain (In my world, if your parents' best friend had a son or a daughter, he or she was automatically your "cousin" by proxy) would hang out for the rest of the night and ride all the rides, play the games of chance like the ring toss and balloon and dart, and, of course, people would be lined up trying their strength at the old ring-the-bell game (I'm told there is a trick to that, but

I still haven't figured out what it is!) One of the things I remember most is not just the sound of the rides or the games or the smell of all the carnival food like the corn dogs and cotton candy, I remember the sound of all those people having such a good time. That was something that stuck in my memory.

The most fun for me was actually the day after the carnival was over. Immediately after the rides were packed up and hauled off, my brother and I would walk down to the firehouse super early in the morning and comb the place for any change that people had dropped or had fallen out of their pockets while they were spinning up there on the rides. I can see that trampled grass right now in my memory like I could reach down and touch it while I'm writing this. We would walk back and forth, back and forth, like we were mowing a lawn with a push mower, being very careful to make sure we didn't miss as much as a square inch as we combed through the grass and dirt for loose change. We collected all the change we could find, and we picked up any bottles we could get our hands on. Back then in New York you could collect bottles and take them to the paper store, and they would give you the five-cent deposit back. It's true... five cents was a lot of money because it eventually added up to a quarter, and a quarter would buy me a piece of candy, a soda, and a pack of baseball cards! The cards came with a brittle stick of pink bubble gum. I can still remember the smell of the powder that would come off of it and the snap as it actually broke when you chewed it. Ahhh, the good ol' days!

I believe the fire department has kept that parade going all these years and that they have the carnival running now for about four days. I'll always have a soft spot for Katonah and for those days with Grandma and Grandpa Dugan. They are some of the best memories of my life.

When my Grandpa Dugan died, it broke my heart because he was my very best friend. It may be a bit morbid to say, but a part of me just refused to believe he was actually dead because I'd seen him in a casket so many times taking a nap or just lying there with me standing next to the casket having a conversation with him. But this time was different. I had to realize he wasn't waking up or getting out, that our days of getting dressed up and marching down Main Street in the parade were over to a close. He had given me this little stuffed tiger, and before they closed the lid, I put the tiger in the casket with Grandpa Dugan to keep him company. I guess somewhere in me I'll always be "Grandpop's Boy."

MAGIC TIMES IN LAKE SUNAPPE

"What's meant to be will always find a way."
— *Trisha Yearwood*

Grandma Dugan saw in the local paper where they had a casting call for *Li'l Abner*. They were having the auditions at the church near her house. On one side of street was the funeral home where Grandpa Dugan worked, and on the other side of the street was this church built out of rock. Getting any part in *Li'l Abner* was a real big deal because *Li'l Abner* was a comic strip by Al Capp that ran in newspapers from 1937 all the way up until 1977. Imagine one of your favorite television shows and multiply the popularity by about a thousand times. It was crazy how everybody loved this strip about the fictional hillbilly town of Dogwood. It was made into a Broadway musical, and then in 1955 Paramount made the movie, so it gained even more followers. Funny thing is that some people still call Daisy from *Dukes* "Daisy May," which was the name of the female lead in *Li'l Abner*. There are actually many places where the characters are similar.

I had been in local plays at the elementary school since I was eight but had done nothing on this scale for a traveling theater company. I went for auditions and gave it my all. Still do. My first time up there on the stage, I almost got the part of Earthquake Magoon. If that had happened, I would have been the best friend to a thirty-year-old playing *Li'l Abner*. I wanted that part, and it never occurred to me not to expect it, even though I was only ten years old. I was already almost six feet tall and weighed right at two hundred pounds. The casting director said, "We actually almost cast you in this part because you're so good, but we just can't do it because of your age." Then she told me one of the most important things I've ever heard in my life, the kind of thing that every kid needs to hear whatever their dreams may be. She said, "You're really good at this, and you need to keep doing it. This is what you're meant to do in life." And I believed her because being in the theater seemed like the most natural thing in the world.

I want you to consider how this little bit of encouragement went a very long way. If you have the opportunity to notice and call attention to someone who is doing something great… do it. You may just change the world with that kindness.

The stage and the sets, the lighting and directors, the entire cast and crew – there was this electric energy, and man, there was nothing like it. I don't know that 'finding your tribe' was a part of the vocabulary back then, but I knew I had found something. That I was in the right place where I was meant to be. I'd love for every kid in the country to have that feeling and be that certain of who they are and what their calling in life is.

From then on out, after the success of *Li'l Abner*, I tried out for everything I could find. I kept my eyes opened for casting calls anywhere and everywhere I could find them. People say there aren't a lot of opportunities out there in life, but there are opportunities everywhere. You just have to look for them, and you have to expect them. It's not like I had someone on the inside or had some special contact to help me get in for the audition. You keep your eyes open, and this part is very important: you have to recognize opportunities and be ready when they show up. That's not the time you're supposed to second-guess your instincts. Do your homework to prepare for your dream. For some kid who wants to grow up and work for NASA, it means studying physics and practicing math problems. And for another kid who wants to grow up and be on the Grand Ole Opry stage, it means staying in your room and practicing that fiddle when no one else is making you do it. My grandparents and my mother strongly encouraged my passions, but they weren't deciding what those were. That passion was original, and it was all mine.

I want to say a word about my dad here. Though he and Mom had been divorced since I was a toddler, I saw him often. Dad was all about being practical. He would say that I needed to have a skill to fall back on in case (read *when*) my desire to be a movie/music star didn't work out. He was probably thinking mechanic or upholsterer. I took his advice and took up magic and the guitar! Years later when I was filming "Dream House," he took me aside and said, "Good thing you didn't take my advice or we wouldn't be here." I loved my dad for his blunt honesty and sense of humor. Miss him every day.

Be prepared, but then be ready to jump. Don't let fear or doubt get in your way. Even though I was so young, the *Li'l Abner* casting crew actually started to cast me in a lead role. This is what you're meant to be doing. So, I got to be a part of the cast singing and dancing in *Li'l Abner*. I remember the girl who played Stupefying Jones. She was a Rockette, and I might have been just a kid, but I still remember her well. Her name was Fern Fitzgerald, and, yes, like all the Rockettes, as the old saying goes, the floor was the only thing that kept her legs from going on forever. So, all of it, the cast, the musical, the rehearsals, the audience, the casting director, it all made an incredible impression on a ten-year-old boy.

I started searching the Pennysaver and bulletins around town for casting calls of any kind. To be a kid who wasn't athletic, who had every reason to be self-conscious or shy, when it came to going after these things and trying out on stage, I was absolutely fearless. There wasn't a shy bone in my body when it was time for me to step up on that stage for a casting call. People say that the fear of public speaking is the number-one human fear. It has been said that I have a fear of *not* speaking in public!

I went on to do all kinds of early theater and musical theater. Every elementary school production I could take part in, I was there. So, singing on stage and being in front of an audience were things I got comfortable doing very early on. I felt like it was the most natural thing in the world. I did as many plays as I could do.

By the time I'd done *Li'l Abner*, I was already into making movies with my Super 8 camera, and I was also getting into magic tricks. Those were the two things I knew would always be a part of my life. John Wayne was my hero, and I knew that somehow, someway, *my name was going to be in lights.* Riding hard, scraping through fist-fights and shootouts, saving the girl, saving the day. I made movies with my Super 8 camera, playing star, director, editor, and writer too.

I have to say it all started with Grandma Dugan and a bunch of Green Stamps. That Super 8 camera was the most beautiful thing I'd ever seen at that point in my life. From the moment I put my hands on it, I knew it was what I was meant to do for life. Maybe I didn't have those words exactly, but there was that feeling in me that you might say was a sense of destiny calling.

The first films I made were taking my Super 8 camera into the funeral home when I was eight years old. I'd been watching movies like *The Mummy* with Boris Karloff, so I thought I was primed for action. I couldn't wait to start yelling things like "Quiet on the set!" Of course, it was pretty quiet already around the funeral home.

Now that I think about it, between Boris Karloff movies and shooting my own movies in the funeral home, it's no surprise that one of my earliest Halloween outfits I created was as a mummified Civil War ghost. This was back in the sixties when Halloween was really a big thing. I mean, your entire school was out on the sidewalks trick-or-treating, and there had never been a scare back then of razor blades in apples or something horrible like that. No one had ever heard of such a thing. So, I'm out there with all of my friends trick-or-treating, and you had to be creative with your outfits because this wasn't during the time when they had fifty plastic princess outfits hanging at the checkout counter or some ready-made Darth Vader helmet and cape. You had to make something up with what you had to work with. The mummy was going great until the toilet paper and gauze I used for wrappings started falling apart. My father had an old Civil War musket, and I used that. It was a great outfit. I knew I'd hit the big time because I landed a full-size Heath bar. They didn't have miniatures back then, so when you got a candy bar, man, you got the full size. Imagine that! It might have been me eating those candy bars that almost got me a lead in *Li'l Abner*.

Then the turning point in my life came when my mother signed me up for something called the Beginners Showcase in Lake Sunapee, New Hampshire. I was twelve or thirteen, and my mother took fifteen hundred dollars she had saved to pay for me to go to this camp. This is 1972, and fifteen hundred dollars was a whole lot of money. She just didn't make that much money as a woman who worked doing flip charts for executives at IBM. For all I know she started saving the night she saw me in that first big role on stage in *Li'l Abner* or maybe when someone in the cast told her I truly had talent and should keep going for it. Mom was committed to helping me realize my dream and trying to get all the training for me she could. She drove me there, and to my delight she left me. Here I was a kid who had never been to camp or even on some sleepover, and I'm at this theater camp in upstate New York. One of the qualities I attribute to the entire experience was this sense of freedom. The drive up there from home was about four and half hours long, and it seemed I was leaving the country. I wasn't just leaving the neighborhood but leaving the state. It felt like it was something majorly important. Like maybe some kids feel the first time they leave home to go to college. Definitely, as if some monumental life change was happening at the moment.

Also, just the drive up there was something to see. I was raised in the city where everything was houses and apartment buildings right next to each other. That's what I saw day in and day out. This was the first time I'd ever been in a place that was surrounded by so many trees. I was going to bed every night and waking up every morning surrounded by the beauty of all that nature. It occurred to me not too long after I'd been on the property in Louisiana, that when I was just enjoying being outside, looking at the lake, the familiar feeling of being up at Lake Sunapee came back to me. That *déjà vu* sort of feeling of being there in camp, and I thought, well, I'll be. I think that's where my love of the land and being in outdoors first came to me. It's also where I fell in love for the first time, but that's a whole other story.

Beginner's Showcase had everything. The camp was exactly what I needed. There were acting classes, yes, but I also learned how to build sets, create crepe paper beards and put them on. We put on the show *Bye, Bye, Birdie* while I was there. The experience absolutely changed my life. Not only did I learn the things that you should do, but also a few things that you shouldn't.

There were some strange actor types there. I remember a guy whose rich parents had bought a class for his broom. Do you hear me? They paid the fifteen hundred dollars for this kid to take his broom to camp with him, and his broom had its own bunk. The broom's name was Joe, but I'll be damned if I can remember the kid's name. That ought to tell you something about what not to do. Sometimes learning what not to do or who not to be like is an important lesson, too.

Even though I was learning so much, it was also a lot of fun in the process. The theater was a big barn structure that seated almost two hundred people, and local residents would come watch the productions. When Alicia and I are shooting movies today and we have the whole crew together, they always comment about how much fun they're having while they're working. I think a lot of that is because we approach it the same way that I had learned to do it in camp. Everyone pitches in where there's a need, and no one is walking around acting like a superstar. People have said, "This feels just like we're at movie camp." That's one of the best things I could hear.

Another great thing about the camp is that they had classes for learning how to perform magic tricks. Before I went to the camp, I was already a big lover of magic. When I grew up, there were just three channels to watch, so everybody knew all of the shows on television. In that era there was Orson Wells hosting a show called *The Magic Circus* on television, and Bill Bixby had a show on called *The Magician*, in which he was a magician-slash-detective. Dunninger's *Complete Encyclopedia of Magic* was something that anyone could get as part of the book-of-the-month club. So magic was very much in the forefront of everyone's mind at that point.

I had my paper route and a shoeshine business in those early years. I'd take my box, my Kiwi Shoeshine Polish and my towel and set it up on the corner of our block. Back then, a kid had to stay in his territory, and that meant on your block you lived on. So, I'd do my shoeshine stuff, and that's where I learned somebody who's all talk and doesn't deliver is 'all pop and no shine.' They pop their little towel and keep talking to you, but they haven't been shining your shoes. I'd hustle up all the business I could muster. I charged twenty-five cents a shine.

Every six months I'd have enough money saved up to finally go down to Tannen's Magic shop in Manhattan. This old magic shop had been around for years. Even if all I could afford was to buy one deck of cards, it was worth the trip to just be able to walk around in there and look at all the wild, magic trick paraphernalia. They had glass cases filled with secret vials and boxes. They had a display of trick handcuffs and padlocks. I stared at those handcuffs long and hard and made up my mind that one day I'd perform Houdini's escape act under water.

There was one guy I met in camp who I wish I could still track down. His name was Paul Moyer, and I ran into him years later at the Magic Castle. I discovered then that while I'd pursued acting, he'd stayed with magic as a profession.

I'm actually a lifetime member of the Magic Castle, the Academy of Magical Arts in Hollywood, California. It's a private, exclusive club dedicated to magic and the art of illusion. Just imagine what it feels like to be a member of a secret magicians' club. This was a long time before the big popularity of Harry Potter, but I feel like a kid again just thinking about it.

While in camp I read the book *Routined Manipulation* by Lewis Ganson, which actually helps in everything including magic, acting, and life. I still love magic, and I'm even better at it now because I have so much experience I can get sloppy with it. The sloppier you are, the better you can be, because while you actually make it look like you're making a mistake, you're performing a trick. You can hide the magic inside the mistake. I'll have to show you sometime how it's done. Well, I'll show you the trick anyway. A true magician can never show you the secret.

Magical Squirrels

• When Lou Tannen started out in business, he had stands all over the city — Coney Island, Flatbush Avenue, and Times Square. The first official storefront was down in the Wurlitzer Building over on 42nd Street. That was way back in the 1940s

• I tried to beef up the squared circle trick once and include fire. Didn't work out too well. Almost set the apartment on fire!

IF I WERE A RICH MAN

"The greatest escape I ever made was when I left Appleton, Wisconsin."
– Harry Houdini

By the arrival of middle school, I'd been practicing magic for a number of years and had gotten good enough with a deck of cards to start performing magic tricks at children's birthday parties. I'd get maybe twenty bucks a show. Eventually, I was able to save up enough money to buy myself an expensive set of cups and balls. Man, they were nice and were made out of brass. These were used for the cups and balls trick, the one where you hide a ball under the cups and you keep moving them around, having people guess which one hides the ball. I also saved up forever to buy the "squared circle." It's a magic box that has a circle in it, and you show people that the box is empty and the circle is empty and then you start pulling things out of it. It's a trick that's a lot of fun to perform.

I discovered Houdini, a cowboy of a different kind. I had a couple of my buddies shackle me with chains and a padlock and push me into the deep end of the pool at our apartment complex. I timed it just as my mother got home from work and had one of my friends run yelling to tell her to hurry and come quick. When she showed up, I yelled, "Hey, Mom, watch this!" Then I had my friend push me into the deep end of the pool.

A big part of magic is showmanship. You have to put on a great show; it has to be entertaining, and since my mother had no idea that I was planning to get chained up that day and pushed in the deep end of the pool, it turned out to be one of my finest performances. People were gathered all around the pool trying to see if I was going to survive or drown. My panicked, screaming mother was the icing on the cake. (*Spoiler alert: I didn't drown, but I do remember Mom saying that if I had she'd have killed me!*)

I was still performing at birthday parties. I also performed in every school play and local community theater I ever had the opportunity to do. I collected issues of *TV Guide* and told my brother, Bob, "One day I'm going to be on the cover." He never downplayed my dream; although, he'd admit to me later he'd thought that my landing on the *TV Guide* cover might be a little unlikely and that he thought collecting TV guides was a strange hobby.

I watched movies all the time, and during this time period, a lot of big hit movies happened to be musicals. I watched them to see how people did things. How they let the music carry them across the stage. The ways that they were really acting even though they were singing while they were doing it. Mom also loved musicals, so we'd watch the old classics as well as whatever was new. Every Fourth of July we watched James Cagney up there singing, "I'm A Yankee Doodle Dandy," and *The Wizard of Oz* was one we watched over and over. *Music Man* was another favorite of ours, and if I was ever tempted to return to Broadway in my life and take on a major role, it would be to play the lead role of Harold Hill in *Music Man*.

Then the show *Fiddler On the Roof* came along. The fact that I played the lead of Tevye in the eighth-grade production of *Fiddler On The Roof* doesn't begin to communicate how much the play meant to me. I had the feeling that I was stepping into a pair of shoes that were larger than any I thought I could ever fill, but when I put them on, they were a perfect fit. With the role of Tevye, even though I was still only thirteen, I was leaving behind the theater experiences of my childhood. When I stepped onto that stage on opening night, and I said those lines, "You made many, many poor people. I realize of course it's not a shame to be poor, but it's no great honor either. So, what would have been so terrible if I had a small fortune?" Then broke into the song, "If I Were a Rich Man." It was like I was no longer playing a role. I was crossing an invisible line between what was and what would be. I was stepping into the shoes made for me, the ones that would lead me down the path and straight into my life.

As fate would have it, Jerry Bock, the man who wrote the music for the play, had a nephew in the cast at the school, so he was in the audience that night for the production. The passion I felt in that role must have come across clearly to people watching. He came up to me after the production to tell me what an incredible job I'd done with the role and how he wished the actor who had played Tevye in the movie and on stage ever since had only been there to be able to see me. All of these words from people like this always meant something to me. It was confirmation that I was doing what I was meant to do.

The next year when I turned fourteen, Mom was transferred by IBM to Atlanta, Georgia. She and I moved down while Bob stayed with Dad in New York. By then I'd had a lot of experience with my Super 8. I'd probably completed a thousand feet of film at that point. I was getting a well-rounded, hands-on education just like I had back in camp. You might not think all of that would add up to giving me a basic education in filming, but it actually did provide just the groundwork I needed. I'd also had years of experience on the stage by then, and leaving town with a rousing lead in one of greatest classical musicals of all time was one heck of a way to pull out of town, riding high on that success. Remember what I said about giving someone a compliment? Thanks, Jerry!

I remember our arriving in Atlanta and just having this big, emotional moment where Mom pulled the car off to the side of the road. She's crying and we're both thinking, *What have we done? We've left everything we knew and the people we loved.* So, on one hand we were scared, but we were also excited about the fact that we were on a new adventure.

Once I got to Atlanta, I immediately joined the drama club at North Springs High. Girls did not find me attractive, and the guys didn't think I was cool. Food and TV were my best friends. I made the Georgia State chorus and put all my efforts into school so I could graduate early and start my show business career.

Back then, I always had a deck of cards or a ping pong ball in my hands everywhere I went. I was an amateur magician and the class clown who did impersonations for a laugh. Oh, and I also carried a guitar on my back everywhere I went. You can imagine how the new kid didn't exactly fit in with the cool kids. In New York I was just the odd fat kid in gym class running dead last in the pack, clutching an asthma inhaler as the other kids got their kicks by pushing me into piles of dog crap, laughing and calling me "Gut."

Even though I don't remember anyone ever being anything but nice to me in Atlanta, you never forget the way that feels. It motivates me to this day -- the fear, the shame, the awkward feeling of never fitting in. No matter how old you are, you're always a kid inside, right? That's also the reason that I connect with kids today and love to share messages that encourage them in positive ways to pursue their dreams.

One of the first things I did in the new school was to see if there were any theater productions happening and anything I could try out for. Tom King was the director, and he cast me in a small part in a quirky little play called *The Curious Savage*. I didn't stand out too much back then except for my size. That was until Mr. King heard me sing when I made chorus, and that changed everything. He chose *Fiddler On The Roof* for the senior production. That was a big deal, and it was assumed a senior would play the lead. Not some brand-new kid who was still in ninth grade. I tried out for the lead, and years later Mr. King told me that he'd gone home that night and told his wife, "I think I've found my Tevye, but he's only in ninth grade."

And she'd responded to him, "I don't think so."

But he just told her, "Just wait until you hear him sing."

So here I was, six-foot-three now and over two hundred pounds in ninth grade, and not only am I the right size with the right voice, I have the lines and the songs already memorized. I have the role down like it was made for me. Mr. King probably took more heat for casting me in the lead than I knew at the time. I'm sure there were some seniors who had been in school productions all those years who figured the role was just going to naturally go to them. He might have had parents calling him to complain because they wanted their kids to get the part, but it didn't matter. He stuck by his guns, and for the second time in two years I walked out on stage and played the role of Tevye in *Fiddler on the Roof*. He tells me the funny thing now is that when he was watching me on stage, darned if I didn't look just like a tired, old Jewish man.

Mr. King became a very special person in my life. Here I was away from my brothers, my dad, and all the family and friends we'd left behind. He became a father figure in some ways, but more than anything, he became a friend. To this day I stay in contact with him, and just a few months ago was able to introduce him to Alicia. He's been to different concerts of mine when I was in the area, and I've never forgotten those early years of being in Atlanta, being the new, strange kid in school and how he helped keep me on the right path and focused on what I was called to do.

I took guitar classes also, but of course I'd been playing the guitar for a long time already, and Mr. King was always appreciative when I'd come into class and sit down to help other kids with chords they were having a hard time with. Or when we were in the middle of play rehearsals that I'd take time to help other cast members learn their lines. These are the kinds of things he's pointed out to me later in life, the moments where he has reminded me about how I had taken some of my hard times in stride and still reached out to be a friend to people or to help others when they were down. To make friends with kids who might be a little different or standing on the outside of the in crowd.

One of my best friends, Patrick Maloof, became one the cast members of *Fiddler on the Roof.* He had played the part of Lazar Wolf. I actually spent one Christmas with him and his family for dinner. Somewhere Mr. King still has a photo of me and Pat dressed up in part on stage and wearing our fake beards, but they looked authentic. The Maloof family made me feel like I was one of them and would have me over for dinner all the time, and Mr. Maloof would say I was just like his son except I was blond and blue-eyed and over six feet tall. They helped me get through that time of being in a new school when my family was so far away in New York, and I was still the strange, new kid on the block. I've always appreciated these people being in my life like the Maloofs and Mr. King when things were still tough for me and my mom, and we were just trying to take it day to day and month to month while making Atlanta feel like home.

School was almost over for the year, and I was looking forward to Bob coming down to spend the summer with us. Little did I know that he was about to say something that would change my life forever.

THE SUMMER I LOST FIFTY POUNDS

*"You can't wait for opportunity to arrive
to start preparing. By that time, it's too late."*
— *John R. Schneider*

Bob had come down from New York for the summer, and we were spending the day at Six Flags over Georgia. Bob was four years older, artistic in ways different from me. Despite our age difference, we had a good time together, taking front-seat rides on the Great American Scream Machine and cranking the wheel on the Drunken Barrels to spin ourselves dizzy. It was mid-May, so the park wasn't crowded, but summer in the South is brutal, and the temperature was ninety-five and climbing.

We'd just cooled off with a massive splashdown on the Log Jamboree, and my T-shirt was soaked and stuck to my skin. "Man, I'm starvin'. You?" I said to Bob. "Let's grab some pizza before we hit the Scream Machine again."

We ducked under a star-spangled hut in the Cotton States section and ordered slices of pepperoni with double cheese. I squeezed into a picnic table, scarfed down a slice in seconds flat and was stuffing the second piece into my face when Bob looked me over and shook his head. "So, I guess you've given up on the whole movie star thing," he said.

"No," I mumbled back, pushing the wad of pizza to one side of my mouth. "What're you talkin' about?"

"How many fat movie stars do you know?" Bob asked with a laugh.

Only one overweight actor came to mind. "Zero Mostel?" I replied.

A mirror ran the length of the opposite wall. I took a hard look. Mouth greasy, filled with cheese. Wet shirt clinging to me, belly hanging over my belt. There was a reason the kids at school had called me "Gut." I had scrawny legs, a forty-four-inch waist and weighed two-hundred and fifty pounds. As a six-foot-three high school sophomore, I was well on my way to the three hundred mark by graduation day.

God bless Zero, but I thought of him because I'd been cast as Tevye in *Fiddler on the Roof* during ninth grade. Mostel made the role famous on Broadway and went on to hit films like *The Producers* and *Mastermind*. Great movies, sure, but I wanted to be John Wayne, not Zero Mostel. I set the slice of pizza down and pushed back from the table.

My life changed that instant, thanks to a long, hard look in an amusement park mirror and a dose of big brother's tough love.

***

A month or so later, Bob and I were at the bowling alley in Sandy Springs, and I was playing the *Space Odyssey* pinball machine. I dropped my quarter, and it rolled beneath the machine toward the back wall. When I stooped and crawled under, I spotted a tiny piece of green paper, folded tight like origami. I picked it up and unfolded a hundred-dollar bill.

"What should I do?" I asked my older, wiser brother. I don't think I'd even seen a hundred-dollar bill before, much less held one.

"What do you think, dummy? Turn it in to the counter guy?" Bob cracked. "You find a hundred bucks, you keep it."

I stuck the crumpled bill into my wallet, and we left. Across Roswell Road, I saw a banner.

GRAND OPENING. NAUTILUS GYM. 3 YEARS - $99.

My brother's words at Six Flags stung, but they had an effect. I was already working on losing weight, limiting myself to sixty carbs a day, switching to Gablinger's, the first (and nastiest) "lite" beer and sticking to the salad bar at Pizza Hut. But I knew that diet alone would not be enough.

The next day, I took my hundred-dollar bill and joined the gym. It was tough walking into Nautilus that first day, knowing I was out of shape. After being picked on by the other kids, I was pretty insecure about my weight.

But even at that age, I understood that dreams require discomfort. There are no easy dreams. Things don't just fall into place; you have to guide, shove, or even sometimes wrestle dreams into reality.

Yeah, I found a hundred bucks. But I could have taken that money and spent it on pizza, beer, and pinball. Instead, I invested it in a gym membership and ultimately, in myself and a career in acting. I still had to show up every day and do the work so that when opportunity came my way, I would be ready for it. Somehow, even at fifteen, I understood those things.

Exercise was miserable at first. But I kept going. Every single day. No matter how tough it was, whether I felt like it or not. By the time summer was over, I'd not only lost fifty pounds, I was in damn good shape.

Now all I needed was an opportunity.

SKIPPING SCHOOL & CLIMBING FENCES: MY MOTION PICTURE DEBUT

*"When you get in touch with God's design for your life,
you know it. But then enemies and well-meaning friends
try to talk you out of going after your dreams."*
— John R. Schneider

"Hey, Rich, what would you rather do?" I asked over breakfast at the A&W Drive-In. "Go to school or be in a movie with Burt Reynolds?"

It was the spring of 1976. My buddy Richard and I were supposed to be on our way to school, but I'd just heard on Z-93 that Burt Reynolds was filming a movie at the Lakewood Fairgrounds. Rich snorted, wolfed down the rest of his curlicues and wiped his hands on his jeans. For two wild-eyed Georgia boys, it was the most ridiculously rhetorical question that one could possibly ask.

Thirty-seven minutes later my white Triumph TR6 was parked in the gravel by the fairground's hurricane fence. "What do we do now?" Rich asked, staring at the barbed wire that topped the fence. Rich was six-two, curly brown hair. Looked kind of like Lancaster in *From Here to Eternity*.

"Way I see it, we got two choices, climb or dig," I replied. "And I didn't bring a shovel," I grabbed the chain-link and pulled myself up delicately over the spikes.

We scaled the fence, dropped down inside the fairgrounds, and started looking for anyone with a walkie-talkie in their hand. Rich pointed to a guy in a Style racing jacket talking into a radio with the antenna up. I ran over and tapped the guy's shoulder. He flinched and spun toward me. I put on my best hurried-but-apologetic voice. "Sorry I scared you, but traffic on I-75 was a bitch, and I'm thirteen minutes late for call time." A veteran of theater since age eight, I knew the most important question to ask next. "So where is hair and makeup?"

A quick lesson for when you're totally lying out your ass:

1. Take the initiative.

2. Be aggressive but charming.

3. Be specific. Use odd numbers. I don't know why odd numbers are more believable, but they are. Just ask the next seven people you see.

Walkie-talkie guy gave me a good once-over and looked at his watch. "I'm Bob," he said, offering a quick handshake. "Hair and makeup's in that trailer next to Burt's Winnie. You want breakfast?"

Rich and I were already jogging over when I yelled back, "Bacon, egg, and cheese sandwich would be great, Bob!"

Another key lesson: Never turn down a free meal. Ever. Even if you're not hungry.

I climbed into the honey wagon and was told to take a seat. The makeup guy had on a cowboy hat straight out of a John Ford Western and one of those vests with a hundred pockets like fishermen or photojournalists wear.

"Close," he told me. I closed my eyes while he put a little powder on my lids. "Look up," he said. I did. He stuffed the powder puff into one pocket while grabbing a brown eyebrow pencil out of another without looking. "Stay still," he said. "This goes on the tear line. Move and it'll go right in your eye."

"Uh, yes, sir," I replied.

With two quick strokes he was done. The pencil vanished as his left hand produced a box of Kleenex. He flipped it over, and there was a mirror cut to the size of the box taped on the bottom. "Good?" he asked.

"Great!" I said. "Love the mirror on the box trick."

"Time is money. Name's Guy Del Russo. I'll be keeping an eye on you on set."

The door to the honey wagon opened. "Breakfast sandwich with bacon, egg, and cheese?" the production assistant said.

The movie, of course, was *Smokey and The Bandit*, a film that would forever influence America and become the second-highest grossing motion picture of 1977. It would've been first – except for this little movie called *Star Wars*.

But nobody knew that then, especially not me. I spent the whole morning waiting to either be put in front of a camera or tossed out of the fairgrounds on my lying a-double-s.

(Squirrel: Nobody ever knows they're working on a blockbuster. Friend of mine worked on a movie that he described as "a fun but small sci-fi movie for kids." That movie was *E.T.*)

Rich and I figured our chances were better if we went separate ways, and I ended up hanging out at what movie folks call the "circus." That's the place where all the trucks and trailers are parked. While waiting, I spotted an older fellow in a tan policeman's uniform. He was sitting in a director's chair next to a red wagon. There was a beer keg on ice in the wagon and a beach umbrella over the top. A kid stood at attention by the keg while the officer drank from a frosted mug.

Seemed like an odd thing for a movie set security guard to be doing. I liked beer as much as any other teenage boy in '76, so I walked over to check it out. "Mornin'," I said. "That beer you drinking?"

The guard was wearing dark sunglasses, but I could still feel his glare. "It sure as shit ain't Dr. Pepper, sonny." He drank the last of his beer and held out the empty mug. The kid quickly refilled it from the keg.

"Beer for breakfast?" I asked.

"Damn hot out here," he replied, leaning forward to blow the foam off his fresh beer. That's when I spotted his name on the back of the chair.

JACKIE GLEASON

Ralph Kramden on *The Honeymooners*. Minnesota Fats in *The Hustler*. THE Jackie Gleason. Here in Atlanta? In a policeman's uniform?

The world had not yet been introduced to "Buford T. Justice," but here he was, in full get-up and spouting his soon-to-be famous pencil-thin mustache and singular brand of one-liners. He didn't seem to mind my hanging around so... "Working hard?" I asked the legend.

"Shit, no," Gleason replied. "Dumb bastard's got me playing a Southern sheriff in some redneck CB radio trucker movie."

Just that quick, he drained another mug and held out the empty. Again, it returned full and topped with foam. The Honeymooner blew it off, and if he cared that most of it was running down his uniform, I sure couldn't tell by his expression. "Where ya from, kid?" he asked me.

The rumor was that Jackie had a summer place back in my hometown, so I took a shot. "Mt. Kisco, New York," I answered.

He remained poker-faced, pondering my response for so long I thought maybe he'd nodded off. But then Gleason broke the silence. "The White Horse."

He was testing me. Fortunately, I recognized the bar's name from an argument I'd overheard when my mom was yelling at my stepdad for being drunk. I replied with the name of another Mt. Kisco watering hole. "The Elbow Room."

Gleason stared at me, deep in thought. Finally, he spoke. "Where do you get your slides developed?"

"Fox and Sutherland," I said, proud to be passing his tests. Then I turned the questions around. "Who makes the best custard ice cream in the world?"

"Nobody but Sam Carvel," Gleason said with a smile.

And just like that, I was in. We were two displaced Westchester County New Yorkers on the set of a film in the Southern summer sun. Common ground, like beer and ice cream, will do that for you.

"How'd you get in here?" Jackie asked, finishing his umpteenth mug.

"I have an agent and a call time," I replied. "I'm in the movie."

Gleason's half-grin told me he knew the truth. He let the silence linger, knowing I'd confess. "I um, heard about the filming on the radio," I said. "I skipped school, jumped the fence, and told the first guy I saw with a walkie-talkie that I was sorry for being late."

Gleason blew the foam off a brand-new beer and took a long sip. "Ever eat at The Goodie Shop?" he asked.

Now it was my turn to smile. "That's where my parents met."

And that's how I made friends with the great Jackie Gleason. For the record, he never did offer me a beer.

***

I had a blast on the set of *Smokey and the Bandit* that day. Actors and crew were on one side of the fence while a hundred or so looky-loos were lined up on the outside trying to get a peek at Burt. It felt good to be on the "in" side for once, tossing a football around and being part of the film.

I hung out with Pat McCormac and Paul Williams (Big and Little Enos Burdette,) met director Hal Needham, and even got my picture made with that infamous black Trans Am. Burt appeared briefly as he walked from a car to his trailer. Word on the set was that he wasn't feeling well, so I figured drinking a beer with Burt Reynolds would have to wait for another day.

Eventually, I was put in the movie. The assistant director actually apologized for not knowing what to do with me and gave me a great spot so I would stand out, between the "Southern Classic" sign and Variety Grill, right next to…my buddy Rich.

"Hey, man!" he said. "Did you know Paul Williams is here?"

Burt remerged to shoot his final bit of dialogue. The race is over, and he radios the sheriff to say he's been chased by the best, and Buford must be part coon dog. For one brief moment, the two put aside their differences to offer mutual respect. Love that part. Bandit reveals his identity and says he's headed to Boston for clam chowder.

"Can you *believe* this?" I whispered, slapping Rich in the ribs with the back of my hand.

Rich didn't even flinch as he watched Burt, Sally, and Jerry Reed roar away in that big red Fleetwood Cadillac. "Sure hate we had to skip," he said with a laugh. "Wonder what they're doin' right now in school?"

You'll find me in the very last shot. Follow the tire that falls off Buford's police car as he takes off after the Bandit and Frog. The tire rolls into the crowd and hits some tall, thin guy on the shin.

Does that guy in the black cowboy hat look a little like Bo Duke? Well, that's because it is. And because the producers chose to freeze this frame and roll the end credits, my three-second major motion picture debut is several minutes long.

Bo Duke in *Smokey and the Bandit*. How about that?

But truth is, Beauregard "Bo" Duke and Hazzard were still a couple of years away.

ACT II:
THE DUKES OF HAZZARD

"I'm not crazy, I'm just colorful."
— Strother Martin in Butch Cassidy and the
Sundance Kid

"We're only going around this circle once,
so we better damn sure have fun on the ride."
— John R. Schneider

THE END FROM THE BEGINNING: JOHN SCHNEIDER FOR BO DUKE

"If acting doesn't work, I'll fall back on singing. And if that doesn't work, I'll fall back in the pool with the chains on."
– John R. Schneider

As I write these words, we are celebrating the 40th anniversary of *The Dukes of Hazzard*. A lot of water has passed under the bridge since *Dukes* began so details are hazy, and the stories tend to come in snapshots and random scenes, kind of like those square spinning flashbulbs on an old Instamatic camera. It's a long ramble through the past, so there'll probably be a few squirrel sightings along the way.

More than a few, maybe. Hell, it might be all squirrels by this point. But slide in through the passenger side window, and I'll take you for a ride behind the scenes of Hazzard County.

***

In 1978; gas was 63 cents a gallon, and the average U.S. income was seventeen grand. *Hooper* and *Grease* were big at the box office while *Happy Days* and *The Love Boat* were popular with viewers at home. And me? Well, I was singing "Stayin' Alive" while wearing a white-fringed spandex suit for a production called *Manhattan Yellow Pages* at the Atlanta Omni International Hotel.

Manhattan Yellow Pages was a cabaret where performers sang everything from Cole Porter to "Copacabana" while the audience downed fancy cocktails and dined on prime rib. I was eighteen, out of school, and doing whatever it took to build my show business resume, from shoe commercials to singing at Six Flags.

The most coveted position at Six Flags was at the Crystal Pistol Music Hall, but those were all taken. My friends and I decided we'd form a barbershop quartet and make our own job. We learned three songs and secured an audition. Before we started, I said, "I sure do love that wandering quartet they have at Disney World." The big boss shot up her eyebrows, and I knew we had our spot.

"Let's hear what you got, boys," she said.

We sang our three numbers. "Six Flags is every bit as good as Disney," Boss Lady replied. "The job is yours. You can start this weekend."

Simple as that. But then we had to learn more songs, at least enough to do a fifteen-minute set before we moved on to another part of the park. Still, fifteen minutes was a much shorter show than the other park performers had to learn.

I spent all summer walking around Six Flags with three other guys in straw hats and matching red-striped suits, singing songs like "Grand Old Flag." It wasn't so bad. I even became a member of SPEBSQSA (Society for the Preservation and Encouragement of Barber Shop Quartet Singing in America.) To this day, the sound of a pitch pipe brings me to attention, ready for "Sweet Adeline."

My first TV ad also took place at Six Flags over Georgia. It was a Fayva shoe store commercial for Cloud Climbers loafers, and I was only the arm candy. The girl had all the lines. ("They're puffed and padded with little clouds of foam!") We shot it on the Scream Machine and ended up having to do sixteen takes in a row. I got so sick that day I turned green as Lou Ferrigno on *The Hulk*.

One week, my agent called with three auditions. One for *The Great Santini*, another looking for a Southerner to replace John Travolta on *Welcome Back, Kotter*, and a third for a project called *The Dukes of Hazzard*.

I thought it sounded like a show about Brooklyn gangs, like *The Lords of Flatbush*, but my agent explained that Warner Bros. was looking for real rednecks from rural Georgia, twenty-four to thirty years old.

"Sorry, John," she said. "As a teenager from New York, I guess that counts you out."

"Hey, I've got an idea," I replied, the gears turning in my mind. "I'm an actor, right? So, what if I *act*?" (Fellow actors, when all else fails... act. But that's another book.)

My agent told the production company I was a twenty-four-year-old Georgia boy. They sent over the sides (a scene from the script to memorize), and as I read about this fearless, reckless, hard-driving, act-first, think-later character, it hit me. THIS. IS. *IT.* I knew the role of Bo Duke had been written especially for me. It was the opportunity I'd been preparing for my entire life.

I was a car guy, studying films like *Bullitt* and *Gone in 60 Seconds.* Hard-driving? That was me, from those first memories of sliding across the ice in Dad's VW to whipping my first little car around the Western Electric parking lot in Sandy Springs. Even though my part was small, I'd been in the biggest car movie of all, *Smokey and the Bandit.* And how did I get there? Because I was either foolish or brave enough to jump a fence and make it happen.

I'd even attended summer school two years in a row so I could graduate early and pursue acting full-time. The signatures in my yearbook didn't say, *Have a bitchin' summer, John.* Instead, my classmates wrote things like, *See you in the movies,* and *I'll be watching for you on TV next year!*

It was as if I could see the end from the beginning. Life had been preparing me to play the part of Bo Duke.

All I had to do was let the producers know. The people from Warner Bros. wanted real country folk, not actors. So, I didn't bring my resume or head shots. I didn't mention that I had been working in theater since I was eight. The *Dukes* audition was at the Omni Hotel, but I did not tell them that I was starring in *Manhattan Yellow Pages* just down the hall.

Instead, I went with my gut. I ditched my tiny Triumph, borrowed a neighbor's Chevy pickup, and showed up to audition in boots and a black cowboy hat, drinking a six-pack of Pabst Blue Ribbon beer.

I took a seat in the casting office and propped my boots on the coffee table. The receptionist shot me a curious look. Seemingly realizing my error, I hopped back to my feet.

"I'm sorry, ma'am," I said, hat in hand, holding out a cold can of Pabst with the other. "Would you like one?" Polite, charming, son of the South. I didn't come as an actor auditioning for the part of Bo Duke. I *was* Bo Duke.

"Uh, no, thanks," the receptionist said. "Do you have an appointment?"

"Oh, yes, ma'am," I replied. "Bo Duke for John Schneider. I mean, John Schneider. For Bo Duke."

I auditioned with a scene where Bo and Luke climb through a window with their bows and arrows, searching for pirated recording tapes. Bo is excited, a little vacuous, impulsive. He's having fun, and I had good time playing the part. (In fact, I did it exactly the same for "Daisy's Song" in episode two of the first season.) Then I finished my beer, got back in the pickup, and drove home to wait for the verdict.

The next day, I got a call to come back and audition again. (In showbiz talk, that's called a "callback.") Same thing. Worn-out boots and black hat. No Pabst Blue Ribbon this time, but I told them I was from Snailville, Georgia, and had just graduated first in my class from the Georgia School of High-Performance Driving.

There is no "Georgia School of High-Performance Driving," and the town is actually named Snellville. Courage? Actor BS? I don't know. But I do know you've got to decide who you're going to be and commit. Casting directors don't know what they want until they see it. You know that saying about how you don't get a second chance to make a first impression? In acting, it's unquestionably true.

Again, I got the callback. In the years before, whenever our phone would ring, I'd say to my mother, "If that's Warner Bros., tell 'em I'm busy."

This time, Warner really was calling. They wanted to fly me to Hollywood for a screen test.

***

I had a first-class ticket on Delta Airlines, three hundred bucks, round trip. Arrive Wednesday, rehearse Thursday, read for CBS on Friday, and fly back home Saturday morning. I boarded the plane with a four-day change of clothes and newspaper stuffed in the holes in my boots.

"Excuse me," the stewardess said. "But aren't you on television?"

"Not yet," I replied, smiling wide as Texas. "But I will be soon."

The Price is Right announcer, Johnny Olsen, was also in first class that day, and he helped me find my way through LAX and out to the Tolucan Motel. The Tolucan sat two blocks from Warner Bros., so the next morning, I walked over and entered through the old gate off Olive Avenue, where Clint Eastwood's office was – and still is.

California clear blue skies and palm trees lining the streets. Long rows of giant soundstages with red lights flashing and numbers on the side, 7, 16, 29. Beyond the soundstages, I spotted a gazebo in a quaint town square and farther off to the right, swinging saloon doors down a dusty road.

Hollywood! I'd made it. Now all I had to do was find out which soundstage was mine.

I stepped inside Stage 14. Several actors were already rehearsing with Gy Waldron, who'd created *The Dukes of Hazzard* based on a movie he'd done back in 1975 called *Moonrunners*. They'd brought out another actor from Dallas named Steve Hanks, and even though we were both competing for the role of Bo, we got along fine.

Catherine Bach was there early on, but the part of Daisy was based on Dolly Parton, so the studio had a bunch of cutesy blonds trying out as well. But there was something about Catherine that none of the others had. Not just the brunette hair, she was... a tomboy. Somehow, Cathy looked like she could change the oil in her Mustang and still be the most beautiful girl in the world. We rehearsed for hours with Gy, and the next day, they sent me over to CBS.

A little background: At this time, America had three networks, CBS, ABC, and NBC. Television was not on demand. You watched a show when it aired, or you missed it.

The race for a network deal was tight, but in 1978, the world was turning toward a dirt road. *Smokey and the Bandit* was a mammoth hit, and Waylon Jennings had just shipped platinum with his *I've Always Been Crazy* album. So, when Waylon signed on to be The Balladeer and write the theme song for a show about fast cars and good ol' boys from backwoods Georgia, CBS jumped in and bought the show from Warner. But that meant CBS also had to okay the cast.

I walked in to find one of those big boardroom tables filled with Hollywood executives whose job is to spend other people's money. CBS President Bud Grant sat at the head position, watching as we tried out. It was a little nerve-racking, sure, but I knew I was in the right place at the right time, so I kept on doing my thing – and made it through the table read too.

Catherine Bach gave me a ride back from CBS and offered a tour of the local sights along the way, driving by the Witch's House in Beverly Hills and showing me around Century City, which at the time was known as the place where they had filmed *Planet of the Apes*.

"See that parking lot?" Cathy said, pointing out a grubby little piece of pavement. "Someone just paid a million dollars for that."

These people in California have lost their minds, I thought. That million-dollar parking lot later became the site of Fox Plaza, the skyscraper from *Die Hard*, *Fight Club*, and *Lethal Weapon 2*. The land is probably worth at least a hundred times that now.

***

We shot Friday's screen test on the set of *The Young and the Restless*. After the test, you wait to hear if you got the part. My agent called the following morning. "Don't go anywhere," she said.

"Do I have it?" I asked.

"No, they're going to read you with other people," my agent replied. "Just sit tight."

We started the process again with new actors. Rehearse, table read, screen test. Then again, the following week. And again, the week after that.

By week four I was rolling into the CBS table read with a "Hey, Bud! It's me again!" Said in my Southern accent, as a twenty-four-year-old redneck from Snailville, valedictorian of the Georgia School of High-Performance Driving. They really believed I was that guy. I did too.

Fifth week, still in rehearsals. Panic set in because *The Dukes of Hazzard* had an order for five episodes and was set to start filming soon. Denver Pyle was signed on by that point, as were Sorrell Booke and Jimmie Best. But they still didn't have a complete cast.

The studio was desperate. Dennis Quaid and Lorenzo Lamas were brought in, and we did every combination of screen test, swapping around. Sometimes I'd do Luke's part so someone else could read for Bo. Quaid played a very intense Luke and was lobbying for his wife, P.J. Soles, to get the part of Daisy -- but no one could compare to Catherine Bach. Lorenzo had just done *Grease* but was not quite right to play Lucas K. Duke.

I was still in my same boots and clothes from week one, and word was, they were bringing in a new guy to try out for the part of Luke. I ducked into a bathroom near the famous WB water tower and saw a guitar case and pair of boots under the first stall door. Back home, I carried my guitar everywhere, and I was missing it badly. "Hey, what kinda guitar is that?" I asked.

"It's a Guild," said the voice inside the stall.

"Cool!" I replied. "I've got a Ventura."

I finished my business, washed my hands, and went back to rehearsal. A tall, dark-haired guy walked in with a guitar. "Hey!" I said. "You're the guy with the Guild!"

And that's how I met Tom Wopat. In those days, studios cast chemistry, and Tom and I had it from the start, the natural give and take that's more than acting, that says more than dialogue written on the pages of a script. Not quite brothers but closer than friends, the perfect connection to play first cousins.

It's not that Tom and I are so much alike, it's because we are different and yet, somehow the same. The show wouldn't have worked if Bo, Luke, and Daisy had been siblings. We had to be first cousins instead. I don't know where you grew up, but you'll usually find trouble far quicker with a cousin than with a brother or sister along. And two cousins finding trouble was one of *The Dukes of Hazzard*'s primary themes.

They filmed our final screen test that Thursday. You can watch it on YouTube. Check out the part where Tom shoots me a sarcastic look and says, "Bo, sometimes your keen mind takes my breath."

I grin back like, *Okay, cuz, I'll punch you later.* That's the chemistry that made Schneider and Wopat the right combination to play Bo and Luke.

While you're watching, take a look at my crazy-looking pants with the black back pocket on the front. That fifty pounds I'd lost a couple years before? I altered those pants myself on my grandmother's sewing machine. Theater background. I knew how to make a costume work.

My agent called with news on Saturday. "John, you're not going home," she said.

"I've gotta do a sixth week of this?"

"Nope, you're doing galley shoots and first pictures tomorrow," she said. "Congratulations. You got the part."

***

Forty-one years later, I'm still autographing the cast pictures we took with our moonshine jugs and cowboy hats in the heart of Hollywood, Griffith Park. The General Lee was photographed with doors open and no number on the side. Sorrell "Boss Hogg" Booke was much slimmer as they hadn't added padding to his white suit yet. (I remember thinking he reminded me of Tom Bosley, the dad from *Happy Days*.) Jimmie Best was there in his black Stetson and Hazzard County Sheriff uniform, looking far more serious than Rosco ever was on the show -- but the studio mostly took shots of Bo, Daisy, and Luke.

As we posed around the General's rebel flag a stone's throw from the famous HOLLYWOOD sign, it struck me that the Duke family was an unusual assembly. Catherine grew up on a ranch in South Dakota; Tom was a dairy farmer from Wisconsin; Denver hailed from Colorado, and I was a native New Yorker. That's right, the actors playing the first family of the South all hailed from north of the Mason Dixon line.

We finished pictures that Tuesday and started shooting the first episode of *The Dukes of Hazzard* the following Monday, back in Georgia, about thirty minutes from my mom's apartment in North Springs.

Random Squirrels:

- Somewhere out there is a screen test of me and Lorenzo Lamas playing Bo and Luke. Lorenzo was starving, and as our scene ends, he rubs his hands together and says, "Hamburgers..." Lorenzo is a great actor and an all-around good guy, but I was like, dude, seriously? We're auditioning for the role of a lifetime, and you're thinking about hamburgers?

- My first car was a four-speed '74 Mercury Capri, yellow with black interior. I made a Super 8 film featuring the Capri called *The Chase*. During the fight scene, we accidently dented the fender, but I told my mother somebody backed into me. You really don't want to piss off a single mom. She believed my story. Until she saw the film.

- The black cowboy hat I showed up in for my *Dukes* audition is the same one I'm wearing at the end of *Smokey and the Bandit*.

DUKES IN GEORGIA: DON'T OVERTHINK IT

> *"Don't ever try and be like anybody else,*
> *and don't be afraid to take risks."*
> *– Waylon Jennings*

In late October of '78, I set up camp in the Conyers Holiday Inn with my waterbed, weight bench, and a video cassette player. Video recorders didn't exist yet, and about the only tapes you could buy were *Butch Cassidy and the Sundance Kid*, *Elvis: Aloha from Hawaii,* and *Citizen Kane.* I bet I watched Butch and Sundance a hundred times. It was almost as if I had Sundance on one shoulder and Butch on the other, passion and perseverance, whispering in my ear. That movie not only influenced my career, but also nearly every aspect of my life and still does to this day.

Six a.m. on the first morning of filming and I was firing arrows from my Martin Warthog bow into a hay bale set up in the Holiday Inn parking lot. Initially, bows and arrows were going to be the Duke boys' main accessory. We were going to carry them everywhere. Well, that got awkward quick. Soon enough, Gy Waldron let us strap buck knives to our belts and stash the bows and arrows in the General's trunk or back seat.

Anyway, back to practice. Twenty-five, thirty, fifty yards. It didn't take long before I was nailing that target every time. Archery had been my favorite back in kids' summer camp, and it was another example of how life had been secretly preparing me for the role of Bo Duke.

While practicing, I spotted a couple of guys standing by three orange Chargers and a yellow Plymouth Road Runner. The Road Runner had a cool black *Starsky and Hutch* stripe down the side, and truth is, I was kind of hoping I'd get to drive it on the show instead.

The two guys walked over to where I was shooting arrows. The taller fellow had a bad limp, so the shorter, blond guy stepped up and shook my hand first. "Gary Baxley," he said. "I'll be doubling you on the show. This is my cousin, Craig. He's doubling Tom."

"Yeah, but I'm taller," I said. "Shouldn't it be the other way around?"

"We're all the same height behind the wheel," said Craig, hobbling up to offer a handshake of his own.

True enough. "What'd you do to your foot?" I asked.

"Shattered it on *Close Encounters* taking the cop car over Mulholland."

Cool! I knew that scene. "Looks like it hurts," I said.

"It'll stop hurting soon as the pain goes away," Craig said with the smirk of a veteran stuntman.

"You do what you gotta do," I said. "Right?"

A van pulled in to take me to where we were filming. Gary and Craig each took one of the picture cars and followed behind. ("Picture car" is the good-looking car they use for close-up filming and not stunts.) We pulled into the Conyers town square so I could get into makeup. There were no trucks and no motion picture circus that day. "Makeup" was simply a director's chair under a tree by the railroad tracks.

Wopat was getting out of the chair as I walked up. I'm a hugger, so I pulled him in tight. "Here we go," I said, slapping Wopat on the back.

"Ready or not," Tom replied.

I climbed into the director's chair. The makeup guy was wearing an old cowboy hat and one of those fishermen's vests with pockets all over the front. "Mr. Schneider, I'm guessing?" he said, glancing at the call sheet hidden in his hat.

"Um, John. Schneider," I confirmed. The "Mr. Schneider" thing threw me. Still does. "But you can call me John."

"Okay, Mr. Schneider, I'm Guy Del Russo," he said. "How about a little makeup this morning?" He grabbed a sponge from his vest with one hand and face cream with the other.

Wait a minute. The hat. The vest. The efficiency.... "Hey, didn't you work on *Smokey and the Bandit*?" I asked.

"Sure did," Del Russo said. "That was back..." He paused, narrowing his eyes. A look of recognition dawned on his face. Then came the smile. "I'll be a sonofabitch! You're that guy who bullshitted his way into the movie!"

What else could I say? "You gotta do what you gotta do, right?"

"Right," said Guy, laughing as the eyebrow pencil appeared in his hand. "Stay still. Look up."

"Goes on the tear line and not in my eye," I quipped.

"You've got a hell of a memory."

"You don't forget your first day on a movie set," I said. "Especially if you're not supposed to be there."

"You do what you gotta do, right?"

"Right."

Just as he finished, the mirrored Kleenex box magically appeared.

"Good?" Del Russo asked.

***

The first scene I ever shot for *Dukes* was talking to Cooter after he flips Rosco's car in the opening of "One-Armed Bandits." Confidence can sometimes be mistaken for arrogance, but I have to say, I didn't feel nervous that day. Playing Bo Duke was a lot of fun. In acting, they say the worst thing you can do is overthink it, and I never did. I was so interested in the process of making a television show that I never got a chance to psych myself out.

One of my favorite scenes came in that first episode. I was sawing a piece of wood to fix the stair rails at the Hazzard County Orphanage. (Why did a town small as Hazzard have so many orphans, anyway?) I gave a speech about fighting the system and choosing the life I was living, not because I didn't *know* any better, but because I believed it *was* better. They weren't just lines of dialogue. I could feel the conviction as I spoke those words.

"You're making too much noise," the sound man said. "We can't record you actually cutting the wood. You'll have to fake it."

Hmm, I thought. *That's interesting.*

So, I pretended to saw the lumber while giving my speech. (You'll notice in this scene that the sound doesn't match the action of my hands.)

"While you're at it," the camera operator added, "don't move around so much."

"Forgive the question," I said. "But isn't it your job to follow me?" I wasn't being cocky, just curious as to how it all worked.

"Yes," the cameraman replied. "But it's your job to make my job as easy as possible. If I can't follow you, you won't be in the picture, and your scene will get cut."

That, I could understand. And that's when I started to learn how to move, and not to move, in front of a camera. Television is a fabricated two-dimensional representation of a three-dimensional world. The only thing that matters is what happens inside that viewfinder. Otherwise, it doesn't exist. My mission was to make what happened in that rectangle as interesting as possible. As an actor or director, how could I do that?

Filming a TV show is like running a race. By the time you rehearse and make it to the set, nobody cares about the storyline because at that point, you're shooting a schedule, not a script. All you're thinking about is that it's lunch time; you have eight scenes to finish that day, and you've shot only three. Eight scenes total equals four before lunch and four after. If you do only three before lunch, that means you have to get five more before you can go home. Television, like most things, is math.

Tom and I enjoyed helping the show stay on schedule. We fed off of the challenge, competing both as a team and against each other. I don't know that it was so much about being a great actor back then, but we were efficient.

It helped that Tom and I both had a background in theater. In theater, you are perfectly free to do exactly as you are told. If you can find creativity within those boundaries, then you can have a good time doing a show like *The Dukes of Hazzard*.

In fact, that's how the hood slide was born.

***

Wopat first slid over the General's hood in episode two, "Daisy's Song." Tom's debut slide is shown over the opening credits of nearly every episode so I'm betting you can picture it in your mind.

In the scene, the cops are closing in as Bo and Luke make tracks out the back door of Boss Hogg's record piracy operation in Atlanta. Luke scrambles down a ridge toward the General Lee with Bo right behind and Daisy waiting in the front seat.

Three choices. Tom can run around the front of the car, forcing the camera to hinge right, losing me and Cathy in an ugly shot. The crew could move the camera back ten feet for a boring shot that kills the energy of the chase. Or, Tom can go straight for the camera.

The only way to do that is jump the car, slide across the hood and hit the window into the passenger side. That's the exciting shot. Watch closely and you'll see the radio antenna snap in two as Tom slides over. He's still got a seven-inch scar on his arm.

But hey, you do what you gotta do…right?

**

It was a cold, wet, Georgia winter that year, but nothing joins people together like a common misery. *Here, you can share my coat. Hey, I brought you some coffee. We're all in this together.*

None of the locals knew who we were, and nobody had seen the General Lee before, so we didn't get much attention around town. Initially, *Dukes* was more of a Southern Gothic-themed show, aimed at an older audience with fewer stunts and rougher language, more like the previous year's hit movie, *Ode to Billy Joe.* (also starring James Best, who's amazing as the bad guy.)

Gangster-types were shooting at us, gunshot squibs going off on trees. Dobermans on our heels, closeups of bared fangs. The Duke boys are wielding hunting bows while Uncle Jesse reminds Bo and Luke not to hurt anyone, just scare them. It's wintertime; everything is grey, and we're shooting off Spring Street in downtown Atlanta. Those early days of *Dukes* were grittier, but later on it became a lot more fun.

**

The entire *Dukes* cast stayed at the Holiday Inn, and we spent a lot of time huddled by the pool, sharing beer and spaghetti or whatever the special of the day happened to be. No actor BS of rehearsal and running lines -- just talking, getting to know one another. I think Gy Waldron set it up that way on purpose, knowing it would help us form the sort of special bond that would come across on screen.

Looking back, that's one memory we all share as important in making *The Dukes of Hazzard* such an extraordinary show. All of us together, laughing and talking around that Holiday Inn swimming pool. That's where we became a family.

Even now, whenever Alicia and I do a movie, we always make time to hang out together as a cast. Sitting around the fire pit, having a beer, eating a home-cooked meal, telling stories. We still believing in casting chemistry, and I'm still falling back on those early lessons I learned while shooting *The Dukes* in Georgia.

One day, I passed by the TV in the Holiday Inn lobby and saw Denver Pyle starring in an old John Ford Western. There were only three channels back then, and somebody switched to the next one. It was Denver again, this time as "Mad Jack" in the new Grizzly Adams Christmas special, "Once Upon a Starry Night." I looked over and there stood Denver, in the flesh.

"What's that like?" I asked, pointing to his image on the screen.

"Well, John," Denver replied, "You know you're in the right business when you can flip two channels and watch yourself age forty years."

I laughed, totally unable to comprehend such a thing at age eighteen. I can comprehend it now. Four decades after *Dukes* began, I can do the same thing.

***

We shot those first Georgia episodes, one at a time, in no specific order, from the tail end of October all the way through Christmas. CBS ended up airing them in the order we shot, mostly because *The Dukes of Hazzard* was scheduled to debut less than a month after we wrapped up filming.

On Friday night, January 26, at nine p.m. Central -- right between *Wonder Woman* and *Dallas* -- America was introduced to the Duke family and their friends and neighbors from Hazzard County. My smiling face is first on the screen, cracking jokes, driving fast, and having fun. It wasn't acting. That really was the life I lived.

Georgia Squirrels:

- That's Guy Del Russo's cowboy hat I'm wearing as I woo Jilly Rae Dodson in the picnic blanket scene from "One Armed Bandits."

- Those three Dodge Chargers I saw on the first day of filming were the legendary LEE1, LEE2, and LEE3. LEE3 was our "picture car" and the one I drove most in future episodes. It was also the Charger we used for those first cast photos taken in Griffith Park. Yes, the doors of these and all future versions of the General Lee actually opened. Only off-camera, of course.

- Tom and I pulled a lot of things out of the General's back seat over seven seasons. Bows, arrows, dynamite, rope, rattlesnakes, babies, fishing gear, tow hooks, tear gas, moonshine, Confederate money, cute blond country girls… The back seat of that Charger was kind of like Mary Poppins' carpetbag after a while.

- The archery target on that hay bale was my acting headshot. That's right, I was firing arrows into my smiling face. Remember, never take yourself too seriously.

- Ronnie Schell plays crooked record producer "Lester Starr" in "Daisy's Song." It was my first time working with someone I had grown up watching on TV, other than our main cast. Ronnie had been on *Gomer Pyle; USMC; Love, American Style*; and a ton of other shows from the '60s and '70s. I was honored that legit actors were lending their talents to our brand-new series.

- Before I returned to Georgia, Warner sent me to a hairstylist in Beverly Hills. My hair was already blond (as seen in screen test), but they wanted it lighter. The stylist pulled my hair through a cap, slapped peroxide on it, then walked away. A few minutes later, some other guy pulled the cap off and rubbed the peroxide through my hair like he was shampooing it. I'm no Beverly Hills stylist, but I knew something wasn't right. Wouldn't that bleach my entire head of hair the color of straw? That's exactly what happened. It took three seasons to get my hair back to its original dirty blond. *Dukes'* line producer, Skip Ward, had to tap my shoulder every few weeks and say "Um… John? The uh, roots. We gotta do something about your roots…" Loved that guy. You can see Skip playing Riptide in TV's *Batman* and as the bad guy in Elvis's beach classic, *Easy Come, Easy Go.*

- We were filming at the Boar's Nest when some dude zipped past in an El Camino and blew his horn, sounding "Dixie." Our executive producer,

Paul Picard, chased him down, bought the horn for twice the retail price, and installed it the General Lee. You couldn't really hear the horn over the roar of the 440, but our sound man recorded it so they could put "Dixie" anywhere they wanted in an episode.

- On that note, the sound man also recorded several takes of Tom and me doing our Rebel yell to be laid into *Dukes* as needed. We're both musical, so Wopat and I gave each one a different tone and pitch. You can hear them back to back in those first five shows. Notice that sometimes a YEE HAA is actually a YEH HOO! Often, the shout sounds out, and our mouths aren't even moving. I guess Warner had no idea those redneck yelps would become as iconic as the characters themselves.

THE GENERAL TAKES FLIGHT

*"It had action yet wasn't violent. It had love for family
and friends but wasn't sappy. We said grace before every meal."*
— John R. Schneider

About a week before our debut aired, *The Dukes* crew packed up and left
Georgia for Burbank, California, and the more family friendly time slot of
eight p.m. I'm not sure why they moved us to an earlier time. Either the
network tested *Dukes* and discovered that kids loved it, or they needed a
midseason replacement for the eight o'clock slot because their brand-new
Captain America series had bombed. (Maybe both?)

Dukes of Hazzard producers finally figured out I was eighteen when
we started production in Hollywood, and I had to register with the Screen
Actors Guild. You weren't even supposed to be working in front of a camera
without a SAG card. Producer Skip Ward brought it up.

"Uh, John, I um…?" Skip didn't stutter, but he spoke in incomplete
sentences. "Heard that uh, maybe, you know. You've been working without
a, um… you gotta have a SAG card and you…?"

"Skip, it cost fifteen-hundred bucks to sign up for SAG," I told him. "I
never could afford it."

"Well, um, John…," Skip said. "You can now."

Skip got SAG to waive my late fee penalties, and I finally became a full-
fledged member of the actors' guild.

***

I wish I had a better memory of the first time I drove the General Lee. It
was probably around the parking lot of the Conyers Holiday Inn. The first
incident I remember clearly is from episode five, "High Octane," the one
where I'm wearing a brown corduroy suit.

I was driving down one of those Georgia red dirt roads in the rain. I
say "driving," but we were being towed behind the camera truck by stunt

driver Richie Burch. All four of the General's wheels were on the ground, and the lighting rig was up on the truck with the camera crew. A few more crew members were tracking us from a van up front.

We were midway into shooting when the General started to fishtail back-and-forth through the mud. Natural instinct is to grab the wheel, but I didn't have any steering. The stunt coordinator's voice came over the radio from the van, "Don't do anything! Let Richie figure it out." Meanwhile, Tom and I were slipping from side to side and sliding rear tires into the ditches. Richie eventually smoothed it out, and we filmed the scene without incident, but it was scary to be out of control and helpless behind the wheel of that big old car.

In Gy Waldron's original script, the General Lee was named "Traveller," and the car was going to be solid grey, like a Confederate soldier's uniform. The producers figured that viewers might not know that Traveller was the name of Robert E. Lee's horse, so they renamed that '69 Dodge Charger F5 Medium Green Metallic R/T Special Edition – "The General Lee."

The "King Of Kustomizers" George Barris designed many famous TV cars, like the Munster Koach, KITT, and the original Batmobile, but he didn't come up with the General Lee. I do believe it was George's idea to paint the Charger orange, (the correct shade is actually Flame Red) not only to make it highly visible, but also because it's a color every mechanic keeps around the shop to paint the engine block and heads after a rebuild.

Early on, I didn't get to drive the General much for the show. They would let me peel in and out of the Boar's Nest, but that was about it. We were shooting in two separate units at the time, so the second unit team was filming stunts while the actors shot dialogue. Nobody was doing those big stunts on television back then. You might see someone catch a little air over a set of railroad tracks or topping a hill in a chase scene, but no one was jumping cars for distance.

I don't believe the first season's script even mentioned a General Lee jump. Initially, the car sequences were going to be more in the tone of Steve McQueen's *Bullit,* but the Trans Am jump in *Smokey and the Bandit* created a huge buzz, and after Craig Baxley went airborne on *Close Encounters of the Third Kind,* they were itching to bring that sort of stunt work to Hazzard.

The first time I witnessed the General Lee take flight was on November

11, at Oxford University in Atlanta when Craig's cousin Gary took LEE1 over Rosco's patrol car. We shot the jump in front of Seney Hall on a Saturday morning so the campus would be deserted. It's the scene from very last part of the show's opening credits.

There's a smaller jump at the beginning of the intro that was done with a two-foot kicker ramp hidden on the other side of a hill on Elm Street in Covington, but for my money, the one over Rosco's car was our first real jump and the one that changed television forever. My mom was standing next to me, and as we watched Gary hit that ramp and soar, I thought, *Holy shit, that guy is crazy*! I never dreamed that I would one day do the same jump over a police car in a General Lee of my own.

Dukes' producers did let me drive through the junkyard in "Daisy's Song" for the scene where we play cat and mouse with the FBI. I wanted to smash into stuff as I was zigzagging through the debris, but those old cars were rusty and stacked high, so the team told me to take it easy. You can kill yourself doing a simple stunt like that. Squirrel break, as I'm watching that scene. I loved the red shirt I'm wearing because it was like Burt's in *Smokey and the Bandit,* but producers said it didn't pop for TV, so I never got to wear it again.

The General Lee doesn't even appear in our third episode, "Mary Kaye's Baby." Bo and Luke drive a blue Plymouth Fury instead. Which ends up engulfed in flames due to a trunk full of 'shine and a dynamite arrow from Luke's Martin Cougar compound bow. I always wondered why we didn't use the General for that episode. Now I realize that the script called for our car to be blown to bits at the end. We couldn't very well blow up the General Lee!

Watching those old episodes reminds me that *Dukes of Hazzard* was a beautiful show. I don't know if people necessarily think of it that way, but our second-unit director and stunt coordinator, Paul Baxley, was a master of cinematic composition. He would either find a gorgeous shot or create one. (Note on Paul: Marine Scout sniper, two purple hearts, a bronze star, dad to Craig, uncle to Gary, and stunt double for William Shatner on *Star Trek.*)

Paul was the kind of director who'd say things like, "At seven-forty-five every morning, there are ducks on that pond. I would love for them to fly away when the General Lee goes by." Paul would then have a tractor move a big piece of gnarled oak into the foreground on the right; the ducks would be in the background to the left, and that Dodge Charger would strike like an orange bolt of lightning, roaring through the middle of a picturesque scene.

Even if you study the car jumps, it's not just a mass of metal flying through the air and crashing to the ground. A General Lee jump was a thing of beauty, a story all to itself. From start to finish, Paul Baxley framed every one of those shots. Every time I place a camera on a tripod, I think about Paul.

***

Gary Baxley flipped the cop car for the opening scene of our first episode, and the battery blew up. After the stunt, Ben Jones had to climb inside to film Cooter's dialogue and got battery acid all over his shirt. Ben wore that same T-shirt for the entire first season.

Watch as the episodes pass, and the holes in Cooter's shirt keep getting bigger. Ben wouldn't let wardrobe replace his shirt because he thought it was such a "Cooter" thing to do. Any decent mechanic is going to get battery acid on his shirt, right?

Ben also figured a hard-working mechanic would have muscular arms, so between takes he would do bicep curls with a cast iron intake manifold. (You can see him flex and show off his work in "The Ghost of General Lee.") Then, he would open the Charger's hood and streak grease on himself to look more authentic. As an actor, I thought that was a cool thing to do to make the part your own.

Cooter's DOG hat? That was Ben's. The studio wouldn't let him wear anything with a brand on it. Nobody wrote the dialogue, "Breaker One, Breaker One, I might be crazy, but I ain't dumb. Cr-*aaa*zy Cooter comin' atcha, come on..." Ben is the one who made up the Hazzard net.

Ben Jones is to *Dukes of Hazzard* what Jonathan Harris was to *Lost in Space*. Harris had a small part in the original pilot, but made himself indispensable, and the producers wrote him in as a stowaway on the *Jupiter 2* so they could keep him on the show.

Ben did that with Cooter. The Duke boys had other running buddies like Brodie and Dobro Doolan in the pilot episode, and had Ben not made his character so unforgettable, Dobro might have been a regular around Hazzard instead. Ironically enough, Ernie Lively, who played "Dobro Doolan," did become something of a regular. He appeared in three episodes as Cooter's cousin, Longstreet B. Davenport, and again in season six's "The Ransom of Hazzard County" as Clyde, the guard. Ernie's family did quite well in Hollywood. His kids, Eric and Blake, are active in movies to this day.

***

During those early episodes, I wore a yellow chamois shirt with cowboy stitching and pearl snaps. Chamois stays wet a long time in the cold, rainy winter, and whenever you see that shirt tucked in, it's because it was buttoned to my underwear. Fist fight at the Boar's Nest? Foot chase down the ridge and through the woods? Flip a car? No problem. My shirt stayed tucked in no matter how intense the on-screen action. (Check out the scene by the creek in "Repo Men.")

It was partially my own fault. I grew up watching a television series called *The Wild, Wild West* and told the wardrobe department on *Dukes* that I wanted to be like *Wild West* star James West. Apparently, TV gunslingers wore shirts that fastened to their underpants, so that's what they gave me.

Every time I threw a punch or made a running jump into the General, I'd crotch myself. I finally took a pair of scissors, cut the buttons out of that contraption, and you'll notice plenty of scenes where that same yellow shirt is untucked. Strange what you remember, isn't it?

***

A few episodes of *The Dukes of Hazzard* had aired by mid-February '79. My brother, Bob, and I went to Atlanta's Perimeter Mall, probably to pick up some new gadget from the Sharper Image store. I'd been going to that mall for years, all through high school. Unnoticed. Until now.

"Look!" somebody cried. "It's Bo!"

The mob descended like I was the Beatles, pulling at my clothes, my hair. It was hard to hide that mop of straw blond hair. Cute girls screamed and pushed pieces of paper toward me, begging me to sign my name. It seemed like the whole mall swooped down upon me, as Brother Bob would say, "to touch the hem of his garment."

Things got so crazy that a security guard had to escort us out of the mall. We burned asphalt as *Dukes* fans clamored for our car, Bob and I cackling like two bank robbers escaping the scene of the crime. "Just think," I told him. "All this because you gave me hell over a second piece of pizza at Six Flags."

As we sped down I-285, I realized that *Dukes of Hazzard* just might turn out to be bigger than anyone had expected.

***

At that point, I was making twelve hundred dollars an episode for those first five we shot in Georgia, and once production moved to Burbank, my pay went up a little more. I'm not bragging or complaining, but after a few decades of *Dukes* conventions, I realize people are curious about the financial side. Each *Dukes of Hazzard* episode cost about 1.3 million to make, which was considered extremely expensive for the time. Once the show became a hit, CBS started charging six hundred thousand dollars for a thirty-second commercial. In one minute of advertising, the network nearly recouped their investment on *Dukes*.

In 1979, CBS built a Friday night that couldn't be beat. *Incredible Hulk* for kids early in the evening followed by *Dukes of Hazzard* for the entire family and *Dallas* for adults later that night. Sure enough, they hammered the competition every Friday for six straight years. (Except for the Coy and Vance era, but that's a story for later.)

People still reminisce about that classic CBS Friday lineup as a beloved part of their childhood and one of the most legendary eras in television history. Often, fans will tell me a story about how they grew up battling a life-threatening illness or struggling with a difficult home life. The one thing they lived for was Friday night. Maybe we weren't curing cancer, but if *Dukes of Hazzard* was able to put a smile on someone's face while they were fighting it, that's worth something, right?

At a recent concert, a woman approached me and said she'd raised three children as a single mom. "I couldn't drag my kids to church, but they sure didn't miss *The Dukes* on Friday night," she told me. "But at least y'all set good examples. Work hard; tell the truth; be generous; always try your best to do the right thing. So, thank you for being a big brother on TV for my kids."

Comments like that mean a lot to me. I grew up watching Clint Eastwood, Chuck Connors, and John Wayne and, in many ways, *Dukes of Hazzard* was like a modern-day Western. We had action, drama, a moral to the story, and in the end -- even though we might've picked up a few scrapes and bruises -- the good guys won every time.

Squirrel Sightings

- *Dukes* was the first TV series to have a full-time stunt team. Eventually, I got to a point where I could do about 73.9% of the driving needed for the show.

- The end credit scene of Bo and Luke being chased around the trees by Enos is an extended cut from the opening of "Money to Burn." The General Lee laps the trees only once in the original episode.

- Richard Petty's wrecked race car in "Repo Men" is LEE1 with some blue-grey paint and a number "71" slapped on the side. After Baxley's long jump at Oxford, it was ruined for anything else. LEE1 was rescued from a junkyard in Atlanta, fully restored, and sold to golfer Bubba Watson. The flag was still there when I signed the car in Arizona. I traded an autograph for a round of golf with Bubba. Sucker sure can crush that little white ball.

- Catherine created the first pair of Daisy Dukes. She wasn't comfortable with the short shorts our wardrobe department offered, so she made her own. Cathy wore pantyhose underneath, so it never felt like she had shorts on while running through the woods or doing the tomboy stuff Dukes required. Daisy is one of the most beautiful women in the history of television, but never seemed to notice it herself. I think that's why the character is so lovable, approachable, and endearing to this day.

- Gy Waldron wanted it clear that nobody in Hazzard meant any harm. Boss Hogg was crooked, but he would never hurt anyone. If Rosco crashed during a chase, the Duke boys always checked to make sure he was okay.

SKINNY DIPPING IN FRONT OF
SIXTY-THREE PEOPLE AND ONE SAXOPHONIST

"The audience will always forgive you for being wrong
and exciting, but never for being right and dull."
— Burt Reynolds

Hazzard Square was built on the Warner Bros. backlot for the 1962 movie, *The Music Man*. Before *Dukes* came in, it was used for John Wayne's last film, *The Shootist*, and afterwards became the town of Stars Hollow for *Gilmore Girls*.

Except for Boss Hogg's bank, the buildings on Hazzard Square were all empty, just frames or fronts that were built on telephone poles. If we climbed the steps and walked through the doors of the Hazzard County Courthouse, there was only a walkway of two-by-fours and plywood on the other side to take us back down to the ground.

Tom did some of the scenes where we would take the mission up high and run across the tops of Hazzard's buildings (as in "Gold Fever" and "The Meeting"), but Russell Solberg, Allan Wyatt Jr., or Jack Gill usually doubled for me. Wopat can't swim, and I don't like heights. Tom had been a roofer back in Wisconsin, so working up high didn't seem to bother him as much – but in the water? Sunk like a rock. No body fat. I still hate him for that.

I love the scene from season one's "Money to Burn" where we're climbing onto the roof of Boss Hogg's Hazzard County Coffin Works. Just as I reach the top, the rope breaks; the action freeze-frames for a cliffhanger cut to commercial, and Waylon suggests that viewers stay tuned to see how things turn out.

It was a close-up shot, so I had to do my own stunt. I was sitting on a scaffold with my legs wrapped around a post so all I had to do when the rope broke was lean back and sell the fall. That's the great thing about acting. You don't have to fall. All you have to do is make the audience believe.

***

There's a part in "The Big Heist" where we tie Enos to a chair and hang him on the wall of the sheriff's station. (Fans might remember me hobbling through this entire episode in ill-fitting mail-order boots.) Union rules said that six hours from the time you start filming, you have to take lunch. Very strict guidelines. If you were in the middle of a shot, and the assistant director called "grace," then you could keep going until the camera ran out of a thousand-foot roll of film, which was about ten minutes. Once the film ran out, it was lunch, no matter where you were in the day. (Remember, we shoot the schedule, not the script.)

We were on "grace" and trying to get the shot with Enos on the wall when the magazine ran out of film. The scene wasn't finished, but we had to break for lunch. Sonny refused to come down. He stayed up there for over an hour. All through lunch.

"The Big Heist" ends with Enos asleep in his chair on the wall. Sonny wasn't acting. He really did fall asleep up there. The director rolled tape and filmed Tom and me waking him up once we were all finished eating. Sonny's a big guy and nearly broke both the chair and wall when we startled him. Don't think that deleted scene made it out to the public, but I made a mental note to never startle Enos again.

In a later season, we wrapped Enos up with police tape in that same doorway. Back then, the crew would snap Polaroids for continuity. Most actors would have removed the tape between takes and let crew members consult the photos to fix it once cameras were ready to roll again. Not Sonny. He stayed tangled up in tape the entire time.

Sonny didn't have a lot of dialogue on *Dukes,* but he would keep his lines on a 3X5 index card in his shirt pocket so he could go over his them again and again. Back in '76, I did a Disney TV movie with Sonny (and Ben Jones) called *Million Dollar Dixie Deliverance.* Sonny Shroyer is an accomplished actor. There was no way he needed cards to remember his lines. But I think Sonny believed that Deputy Enos Strate would need those cards so that's what he did.

Remember the story of how I auditioned for the part of Bo Duke wearing a cowboy hat and carrying a six-pack of Pabst Blue Ribbon beer?

That spark of inspiration came from a legendary story I'd heard about a Georgia actor who got so into character that he spit tobacco juice on the floor during an audition. That local actor was Sonny Shroyer.

Sonny is still a bit of a wild card. Crazy, delightful – one of my very best and beloved friends. But to this day, I'm never quite sure when he's serious or just pulling my leg.

***

There were sixty people on *The Dukes of Hazzard* film crew, so anytime it seemed like Bo and Luke are way out in the country alone, there was actually a big crowd of people, lights, and cameras gathered around. Occasionally, we'd have to shoot some of the rural scenes out in public.

We would get cursed at and flipped off whenever filming around Los Angeles. The locals would petition to keep us from shooting in their neighborhoods. The Duke gang was not well-loved in California. It was more like, *oh no, that damn hillbilly car show is back again....*

Some saw our presence as a nuisance and others as an opportunity to make money. In "Deputy Dukes," Cindy Lou and Maybelle, two cute and conniving girls, trick Bo and Luke into going skinny-dipping before running off with their clothes and the hundred dollars they'd won in a snipe hunting contest. (We got snookered again while skinny-dipping in "The Ghost of General Lee." You think we'd learn?)

We shot the scene for "Deputy Dukes" in an area off of Coldwater Canyon up in the Hollywood hills. It looks remote on TV, but the location was quite populated. I remember passing Marlon Brando's house on the way to the set that morning.

There was a local fellow who made his living by finding out where the studios were filming, showing up nearby, and practicing his saxophone. One of our production assistants finally went over and paid him to stop with the sax so we could continue shooting Bo and Luke's skinny-dipping scene.

No, Tom and I were not really naked. Freeze-frame the right moment, and you can tell that we're both wearing shorts. (Google "TreePeople Coldwater Canyon" to see photos near our swimming hole.)

Earlier in the episode, Cindy Lou and I are making out in the back of a beautiful red and white Mercury Cougar convertible. Shortly after we wrapped, the crew dropped a dumpster on the Cougar's hood and nearly totaled it. Ouch. Just a couple of small reasons *The Dukes* was such an expensive show to make.

***

Fans often ask what my social life was like outside of *Dukes of Hazzard*. Well, I didn't really have one. Everybody partied more than I did because all I did was work. I even worked on the way to work. (Still do.)

Five days a week, we were on set for six a.m. call, and we worked late most every night. Every weekend I was out to a car show or autograph signing somewhere. In addition, at nineteen, I opened an auto repair shop next to Dick Clark's office called Celebrity Machines where we worked on exotic cars, mostly Ferrari, Lamborghini, and Maserati.

I would do a few botched paint jobs here and there, but I was much better at taking cars apart than putting them back together, so a mechanic from South Africa named Gary Kirsten did most of the serious repairs. Celebrity Machines was mainly a good excuse for me to buy fast cars and keep them for my own amusement.

Once, in the early days of *Dukes*, Gary and I flew out to San Jose on PSA Airlines. I had a Colt 45 in my duffel bag along with twenty thousand dollars cash and another 2K hidden in my sock so I could buy a 1975 Maserati Bora, fire engine red with a black interior and stainless-steel top.

I drove the Bora back, blew a head gasket and coasted all the way from Frazier Park to Newhall Ranch. I had to shoot *Dukes* at sunrise the next morning, so I left Gary to ride in with the tow truck and called a taxi so I could get to work. Pistols and piles of cash on commercial flights. Man, those were different times.

***

By the second season, I was driving the General Lee a lot more often. Things at the studio were lax, and I could come in after hours and take the car. When I say, "the car," by that point there were fifteen or twenty General Lees lined up on the Warner Bros. backlot.

Figure a hundred and forty-seven episodes, wrecking at least two

Chargers per show…so we had over three hundred in all. (Even with the miniatures, which we'll get to later.) The crew demolished at least that many patrol cars, which were mostly Furies or Dodge Monacos or Matadors since they were cheap and plentiful at the local police auctions.

Back to the story. You could start just about any vehicle on the Warner Bros. lot with a flat-blade screwdriver, so I'd borrow one of the Chargers to "practice" and tear ass down by the docks on the Los Angeles River or burn through the studio backlots while taking my buddies for a ride.

Once, I grabbed a friend and jumped in one of the second-unit Generals. The stunt team's Chargers were tricked out with the hot rod 440 Magnum, so I tore up and down the backlot's dirt roads, sliding and kicking up storms of dust. I came back to one seriously pissed-off studio executive.

"Didn't anyone tell you that we're shooting *Honeysuckle Rose* this week?" he fumed. "Every time they roll camera, the General Lee roars into the shot."

As much as I would've loved to have met Willie Nelson, that probably wasn't the right time. Shaking hands with the Red Headed Stranger would have to wait.

As I got more experience behind the wheel of the General, and the producers realized I was capable, they started letting me do more of the stunt driving, the "bootlegger" 180s, gunning into Hazzard, and skidding sideways in front of the sheriff's station before we run inside. Then we'd dash back out, jump in, and I'd fishtail out of town. I could do pretty much everything except drive on two wheels and make the jumps.

One morning we shot a scene where I speed up to the farmhouse, hop out of the General, and head in through the back door. Later that afternoon, someone from catering said, "Hey, John, how was lunch?"

"Great," I replied. "I love fried chicken."

"Glad you liked it," they said. "'Cause you ran over that chicken on the way in."

Oh, well. Thank God, I never hit Maudine.

***

In the story before *Dukes* began, Bo was a stock car driver. There are two main members on a NASCAR team, the driver and the crew chief. Luke was the brains, so that's how I became the primary driver of the General Lee. You would never swap roles in the racing world, so for the most part, we kept it that way on *Dukes*.

Our system for those lightning-quick getaways developed over time. Tom was athletic, but I'd never played sports a day in my life. Early in the series, you'll see him look back and call, "C'mon, Bo, hurry up!" He finally figured out to go slower, at least until we got to the car.

Tom would brace himself on the roof, hop up and slide straight into the passenger side. My arms are long, so I'd plant my right hand on the quarter panel, scissor-kick both legs toward the window, and use my left hand to pull myself in by the door frame. The General had a full roll cage at first, and that old steering wheel was enormous, so it was hard to slip inside without banging my elbow or knees. Another key factor in sliding through the window of a car: remove the door lock knobs first. They're flush in newer vehicles but a classic Dodge Charger's lock knobs were flared pegs of steel that would snag a fellow's good ol' boys in a flash, if you know what I mean. If not, well, try it for yourself and you'll soon find out. Anyway, let's move on.

Tom would slide in first, start the General (keys stay in the ignition, country boy) and jam it into low gear just as I'd land with my foot on the gas and hands on the wheel, ready to hightail it out of there. We became so pit-crew quick and polished that the General's tires would be burning before my butt even landed in the seat.

Later in the series, the producers called for more scenes with Luke driving. I don't think Tom complained, but maybe his stunt doubles wanted a chance behind the General's wheel. We would shoot a sequence where I'd drive into Hazzard, we'd get out at Rhuebottom's Dry Goods, and then Luke would drive back down Old Mill Pond Road to the farm.

It didn't make much sense to have us keep switching out, and in addition, I was so used to sliding into the driver's seat that it was awkward for me to get in on the passenger side. Tom wasn't nearly as graceful sliding through the opposite window, either. It was like a right-handed pool shark forced to play leftie against Chickasaw Slims.

One day, we were shooting a scene on Hazzard Square with Tom driving. I had to run and jump into the passenger side so we could make a fast exit. A group passing through on the Warner Bros. tour had stopped to watch our take. Who doesn't love performing for an audience?

"Roll tape and... action!" the director called.

I hoofed it down the courthouse steps, took a flying "Bo Duke" leap, kicked both legs toward the General Lee's window – and missed. My rear end smacked the door frame, one foot in the well and the other in the wind, arms flailing, fumbling for a grip on fresh waxed Charger steel. I fell backwards onto the sidewalk, boots in the air and the tour group erupted in laughter.

"Cut!" the director cried.

Oh, well. So much for pride.

Reversing roles caused more than a few screw-ups. You'll be watching a scene where Bo is driving, then the camera cuts to Rosco and Cletus in hot pursuit. When they come back to the General, Luke is suddenly at the wheel. What happened? Did we switch positions mid-chase?

Another reason to stick with the same driver is that if the General Lee is traveling right to left, you'll always see my yellow shirt behind the wheel. And if it's moving from left to right, you'll see Tom's blue plaid shirt on the passenger side. That way, any driving footage can be used for any show, at any time.

Which answers another common Dukes question: *Why did Bo and Luke never change clothes?* Because it helped with continuity and enabled us to reuse shots from year to year. It was simpler to wear the same clothes every episode.

Once the producers landed on my yellow shirt, they kept it for the rest of the series. Again, that's a holdover from Westerns. Notice that the stars of *Bonanza* rarely changed clothes. It made shooting and editing easier and simplified the process of filming a schedule... um, I mean, show.

There was a lot of action in Hazzard between bar fights, car chases, wood-chopping, fence-mending, and post hole digging. Our clothes got dirty. Even poor farmers don't wear the same thing every day. Tom and I always wanted to poke fun at our outfits with a scene that showed seven identical yellow "Bo" shirts and seven blue plaid "Luke" ones hanging on the Duke family clothesline. But we were shooting a tight schedule and never got the chance.

I keep wardrobe changes to a minimum in my films to this day. It helps eliminate mistakes. For the murder/courtroom thriller, *Inadmissible*, I wear the same suit for the entire movie. Even in the scenes with the punching bag, I'm wearing those seersucker pants and fancy shoes with red laces.

Season Two Squirrels:

- Sorrell Booke wore a black robe between takes to keep Boss's white suit spotless.

- Tom accidently knocked out actor Gerald McRaney while filming "Hazzard Connection." We were shooting in a cave, and Gerald was doing his own fight scene. Stuntmen know to move away, but Gerald leaned into Tom's punch and got waylaid. By the way, McRaney was an early consideration for the part of Luke.

- I played a Union solider in Disney's *Million Dollar Dixie Deliverance*. "I got the dogs, sir." That was my one line. I met Ben Jones and Sonny Shroyer on set. Sonny had just done The Longest Yard, and both were local legends. Sonny and Ben also had parts in *Smokey and the Bandit*. Legitimate parts. As in, they didn't have to climb a fence.

- The first car I bought with *Dukes* money was a powder blue 1979 Porsche 911 SC. $24,000, brand new. My manager convinced me it was cheaper if I bought two, so he ended up with a new Porsche, too. Pretty slick, huh?

- During one of my impromptu driving "rehearsals" on the Warner backlot, I came screeching around the street where Boss Hogg lived and threw a 180 in the wide spot in front of the gazebo, only to find seventeen SWAT team members pointing their weapons at me. I didn't know that Warner rented Hazzard Square to the LAPD for tactical drills on weekends. We all laughed, I signed a few autographs and didn't get shot or thrown in jail. Still, the outlaw in me wonders what might have happened if I'd have pulled out my Warthog bow?

- Allan Wyatt's train jump for "Granny Annie" set a *Dukes'* distance record at 230 feet. The impact killed Al's brakes, and he had to steer into the back of a ten-ton truck to keep from running into traffic.

- Interesting to note that *Dukes* debuted in the era of a Democratic president who, as a farmer from South Georgia, exemplified Hazzard values. His Republican successor was an actor who had cut his teeth on Hollywood Westerns. I like to think that our universal success lies somewhere between both appeals.

SMALL TOWN FEEL

"We built the castle, and they're stealing the furniture."
— James Best

If you ever see the Dukes dangling over a cliff or up on a hilltop, it's likely that we did those scenes over at Indian Dunes, a popular location for filming projects like *The Mod Squad, Escape from New York,* and *Baa Baa Black Sheep*. It was freezing in the morning and blistering hot most afternoons, but you could film up high without any signs of the city behind you.

We shot all of *The Dukes'* airplane sequences up at the Dunes landing strip. We needed a single-engine plane on the plateau for the hijacker scene in "Officer Daisy Duke," and it was really windy that day. The stunt pilot brought in an airplane, landed on the plateau, and promptly flipped it. An ambulance took the pilot to the hospital (he was okay) while our crew dragged his plane out and called in another plane and pilot.

The second pilot arrives and looks over the airstrip. "That guy must've been an amateur," he boasts. It's part of any stuntman's job description to be a little cocky. "No problem!"

The second stunt pilot jumps in his plane, certain he can pull off the gag. So sure, that *Dukes* location manager Jim Molhmann climbs in the passenger seat with an envelope full of cash so he can pass out daily per diems to the second-unit team waiting to film at the airstrip.

Mohlmann and the stunt pilot make a wide loop and come in for landing up top. While taxiing, the pilot clips the dirt rim of the airstrip and flips his plane tail over nose. A gust of wind carries it off the plateau and into the gorge. Plane number two is down, and our location manager is in it with a fat stack of cash.

All we can do is watch as the tiny craft tumbles slowly through the grass and comes to a rest against a cluster of brush below. Suddenly, we see movement. Crusty Jim Mohlmann climbs out of the plane and crawls back up the hill.

"All right," Mohlmann growls, pulling out a wad of bills. "Who needs their per diem?" If you worked on *Dukes*, you had to be tough.

Our production team pulled the first plane down the runway to film the kidnapping scenes. Since the wings and prop were already crumpled, they cut to a close-up to show the "wreckage" from Luke's dynamite arrow and Daisy's sabotage. Sometimes you improvise. We got the shot on schedule, and it was a good example of everyday life on the set of *Dukes of Hazzard*. It's worth saying again: you do what you gotta do.

It was this same ravine at Indian Dunes where I crashed Daisy's Road Runner for season two's "The Runaway," right before she gets her Golden Eagle CJ-7 Jeep. If you play that scene in slow motion, you'll see a head pop up just as Bo and Luke jump out of the car. I think it was stuntman Jack Gill, who hit the brakes after we bailed, and Russell Solberg, who doubled me jumping out for the wide shot near the edge.

The second team came in, sent the Road Runner over the cliff, and we set it on fire for filming. The charred remains of that yellow Plymouth sat crumpled at the bottom of the ravine for years after that crash. I wonder who ended up with the remains of Daisy's original car?

For behind-the-scenes fans, by season two we were using a '71 Plymouth Satellite with a black stripe painted down the side to match the Road Runner. And yes, sharp-eyed viewers, the ghost of Daisy's car appears in a few episodes even after it was crashed. Believe it or not, I never realized that until researching this book.

The stunt team filmed Gary Baxley's record-breaking General Lee jump over the Santa Clarita River at Indian Dunes for the season one finale, "Double Sting." That jump was so iconic that *Dukes* producers ended up using the footage in several future episodes as well as adding it to the opening credits of every season thereafter.

It was a beautifully composed shot, a brilliant orange Charger soaring across the open sky, red dirt streaming from the tires like a rocket trail. Again, the genius of Paul Baxley.

Shortly after we shot that jump, a helicopter crashed at the same location on the banks of the Santa Clarita while filming the movie *Twilight Zone*, killing Vic Morrow and two child actors. Filming at Indian Dunes ended, and the land was eventually turned back to farming.

***

In the final scene of "Officer Daisy Duke," you'll see Bo standing in the Boar's Nest next to a blond fellow wearing a white apron. We're about the same height, and you might even notice that we kind of look alike. That's my stand-in, Jim Kindelon, who also played the bartender.

Cathy and Denver's stand-ins were often used as regulars at the Boar's Nest as well. Stand-ins are not the same as stunt doubles. They watch the rehearsals, and afterwards, the camera assistant will put pieces of colored tape on the floor so each actor will know where to stop walking and the camera operator will know where to focus. First team goes away, and the stand-ins come in and go through the movements so the cinematographer can set the lights while we're getting our makeup touched up, doing interviews, or enjoying a Boar's Nest beer.

We used the same crew, same stand-ins, and same stunt team for the entire run of the show. We even had the same background extras and cars to create that small-town feel. If you live in a small town or grew up in one, you know what I mean. Day in and out, you see the same people at the stores and in the streets. You know who drives the white Ford pickup and whose Monte Carlo burns oil. Even if you don't agree on politics or religion or much of anything, they're your neighbor, and you look out for one another.

I believe viewers picked up on that, and it was part of the reason we were successful then – and why the show still endures to this day. For a lot of folks, the Dukes were like family, and Hazzard felt like home.

***

Jimmie Best walked away during season two over a dispute about working conditions. Seems like every other episode, they'd throw him in a mudhole, horse trough, or Hazzard Pond. Jimmie didn't mind doing it – but could he at least have somewhere to shower and change after they crashed Rosco's patrol car into a vegetable stand and covered him in tomatoes? Jimmie would have to stand off to the side while two crew members held up blankets and a third would hose him down.

Jimmie Best was fifty-five years old at the time and a legendary acting coach and star of stage and screen. He deserved better treatment at that point of his career, but instead of giving Jimmie his own motor home, producers decided they would fill the role of Hazzard's sheriff with someone else.

Bewitched's Dick Sargent was one of the replacements. He was a delight to work with but didn't have a clue about how to approach the role. As Sheriff Grady Byrd he tried too hard to be Rosco and lasted only a couple of episodes. (Billy Asher, director of *Bewitched,* also directed "Road Pirates" and "Deputy Dukes." Not sure if he had anything to do with Sargent's coming in.)

Clifton James from the Bond movies played Sheriff Lester Crabb for "Treasure of Hazzard," and James Hampton from *F Troop* stepped in as Sheriff Buster Moon for an episode as well. I was surprised they didn't simply bring back Hatchapee County's Sheriff Spike Loomis. Spike had already been introduced to viewers in season one, and the actor who portrayed him was our location manager, Jim Mohlmann. ("Who wants their per diem?") Jim was an intimidating guy, big as Don Pedro, who played Sheriff Little.

Eventually, the studio caved and gave Jimmie a modest place to change. For his first episode back, they put him in the pond again.

I didn't fare much better on accommodations. I inherited actor Alan Ladd's old dressing room. It was twelve by twelve, with no bathroom and a record player that was covered in dust because, well, the last person to use it was Alan Ladd, and he'd been dead nearly twenty years. (No disrespect to Alan. Loved his work in *Shane* and *This Gun for Hire.*)

I had that same dressing room for the entire show. It didn't matter to me; I'd rather be outside on the set. Tom and I usually worked from the first shot in the morning until dark so there wasn't much down time to hang out in a dressing room anyway.

Then again, they weren't always throwing us in Hazzard Pond…

***

Jimmie Best was not a particularly comical man off set. Sorrell brought out Jimmie's humorous side as they would antagonize each other in the best possible way. Most of their scenes together were improvised, and it got to the point where *The Dukes* writers wouldn't even try to create dialogue for Boss and Rosco. They would lay out a general direction and let those two have fun. I believe that's how they became one of television's classic comedy teams.

After Jimmie got a motor home, he brought his watercolors and would set up an easel and paint the scenery around Hazzard when he wasn't required on set. You could tell that painting brought Jimmie peace, as did practicing martial arts.

It was a little strange to see Jimmie doing those kata moves in his Rosco P. Coltrane uniform, but turns out he was a black belt in Karate. Jimmie had served as an army MP during World War II and kept himself rock solid. When you watch the physical comedy he did on Dukes, you can see that Jimmie had to be in great shape.

One of my favorite Jimmie Best stories is from back in Georgia. The makeup chair was outside, and Guy Del Russo would hold his hat up to block the sun while he worked on our eyes. But we would be talking and moving around too much, so Guy finally put a picture of a pinup girl inside his hat for me and Tom to look at while he worked on our faces.

"Hey!" Cathy protested. "Now, how is that fair?"

Jimmie took a Polaroid of himself in classic Rosco pose wearing hat, boots, gun belt – and nothing else. The next day, Jimmie slipped the photo into the top of Guy's hat. Catherine sat in the makeup chair, and Guy held it up to block the sun.

"OH, MY GOD!" Cathy screamed. "JIMMIE!!!"

***

Catherine Bach could be shy and kept mostly to herself on the set of *Dukes*. She was going through a divorce from Angela Lansbury's son, David, at the time so I'm sure she had a lot on her mind.

A stylist used to follow Cathy around to make sure her hair had just the right amount of shine and bounce, and when she wasn't on camera, she'd have curlers in the size of beer cans. I used to tease her by asking, "Can you pick up more channels with those?"

Fans seem curious, but truth is, our relationship was always platonic, just like on the show. Sure, you realize your first cousin is gorgeous, but you can't think of her in any sort of romantic way.

Besides, we were too busy working. Viewers see our on-screen chemistry and think filming *Dukes* was like hanging out with your buddies – but that's why it's called acting. Sometimes it was fun, and for the most part, we all got along well. But it was work. First priority was to hit our marks and keep the show on schedule.

Tom and I were always in the General Lee, so we had plenty of time to BS between takes. Cathy and I didn't have that. The only quality time we got to spend together was outside of L.A. at events like parades and car shows.

Once, during the peak of *Dukes*, Cathy asked me to be in some small-town parade, promising that a hundred thousand people would show up. "Cathy, your curlers must be in too tight," I replied. "There's no way that many people will turn out. But yeah, I'll be there."

Well, sure enough, Catherine was right. A massive crowd descended on this podunk town in the middle of Vermont. Cathy and I rode in the parade, shaking hands, taking pictures, women screaming and handing us their babies to kiss. We felt like Burt and Dolly at the Hazzard County Fair.

Catherine really was a small-town girl, coming from a tiny place in South Dakota called Faith. Whenever she would have friends visit from back home, they were every bit as sweet, beautiful, and charming as she was. I don't know what's in the water back in Faith, but in my mind, I always pictured an entire town full of Daisy Dukes.

Small-Town Squirrels of '79:

- Catherine's stand-in, Maryellen Aviano, dated Tom for the longest. If Maryellen was in the corner of the Boar's Nest tapping her foot, that meant Tom was in trouble. Maryellen was a sweetheart, so we knew it had to be Wopat. M.E. (that's what we called her) runs J.J. Abrams' Bad Robot Productions these days and was casting director for the recent *Star Wars*.

- Look on the General's passenger side during Gary's river jump and you'll see a camera in an iron box. No attempt was ever made to hide it, and nobody seemed to care. Even though that jump was high and far, the Charger landed in the sand and drove away.

- Tom and I were shooting a scene in a hayloft looking down at the bad guys with the camera over our heads. Wopat wore glasses back then, and just before filming, he'd take them off. There was an electrical junction box to his right. He set his glasses on top, hit both poles, and they instantly melted. Cut! Tom went to contacts after that but had a hard time on those dusty country roads. I can still see Tom on set, pulling out a contact and sloshing it around in his mouth to wash off the dust. Contacts never worked for me. I like the world the way I see it.

- They really let me wrestle an alligator for "Treasure of Hazzard." Her mouth was taped shut, but I've still got scars on my chest from the ridges on her back. Paul Baxley had a special tank brought in and stood outside yelling directions at me. I never heard them until I watched the dailies the next day. It never occurred to Paul that I couldn't hear him underwater.

- In December '79, I drove a motorcycle through a ring of fire for *Circus of the Stars* and joined Dick Clark to co-host *New Year's Rockin' Eve*. That Christmas, I surprised my mom with a brand-new Mazda RX-7. Rich, my *Smokey and the Bandit* schoolmate, drove it from California to Georgia for me. I'd bought a house on Mount Vernon in Atlanta, and we sneaked it into the garage with a big red ribbon on top.

- Never did see that Jimmie Best Polaroid. From what I hear, our sheriff was packing.

LOST SHEEP TO SHEPHERD

*"The purpose of our gifts is to serve others. God gives
you the tools to build someone else's house, not your own."*
— *John R. Schneider*

We filmed our first few years of *Dukes of Hazzard* at Disney's Golden Oaks
Ranch out on Placerita Canyon. Disney Ranch is a nine-hundred-acre
location where they had done rural shows like *Little House on the Prairie* and
The Apple Dumpling Gang. That's where we shot Uncle Jesse's farmhouse,
the Boar's Nest, and all of the country road scenes.

You'll notice in those first seasons, everything looks meticulously
groomed, like a golf course. Needless to say, Disney was none too pleased
about cop cars and Dodge Chargers tearing through the countryside. They
wouldn't even let us park our catering truck on the grass. Still, it was pretty
incredible to be working at the place I'd watched on TV as a kid.

The Boar's Nest is nestled on a hill, and if you look closely, occasionally,
you'll spot a peacock. Disney Ranch was famous for its peacocks, and
they were a total pain during filming. God forbid, I'd have cut wide on a
curve and run over a Disney peacock with the General. *Dukes of Hazzard*
might've been cancelled in season two.

We weren't even supposed to shoo the peacocks away, but when one
would roost on the roof of the Boar's Nest, we would gently toss pebbles up
to get them out of our shot. (Note to Disney: *The Dukes* cast did *not* throw
rocks at your peacocks. We tossed pebbles. Gently.)

Disney Ranch was the location of the covered bridge that appeared in
several episodes such as "Granny Annie" and "Find Loretta Lynn." It was
also featured on *Bonanza, The Greatest American Hero,* and it's the same
bridge that Kid Rock races his bad-ass silver Trans Am across in *Joe Dirt*.

Die-hard *Dukes* fans still ask me about jumping off that covered bridge
from the back of Cooter's tow truck in season two's fifteenth episode,
"Follow that Still." I wish I could take credit, but it was actually my stunt

double, Allan Wyatt Jr. who made the leap. I just waded in and surfaced for the camera.

Again, notice Paul Baxley's composition of the shot. Alan swan dives from a moving vehicle through a gap between the bridge rails and splashes head-first into the stream. As he hits the water, a flock of mallards takes flight. Beautiful.

People often want to know which *Dukes of Hazzard* episode was my favorite to make. Well, we shot that one at Disney Ranch, too. Riding high on season two's smash ratings, CBS premiered the first *Dukes of Hazzard* TV special.

It was also the first episode to feature Duke against Duke.

***

"Carnival of Thrills" was a two-hour special that debuted on Sunday night April 20, 1980, opposite the television premiere of *The Sting* on ABC. Robert Redford was a hero of mine, so when *Dukes* won the ratings that night, it felt like I had arrived.

I particularly enjoyed filming Bo's fight scene with Luke for this episode. John Wayne had just passed away, so Tom and I wanted to do our fight like Wayne and Montgomery Clift in the 1948 classic, *Red River*. Unless it involved some really wild stunt, Tom and I performed all our own fights, which was a big help because the cameras could get in close to the action.

Seems like every episode of *Dukes* had a fight scene, but Tom was a born athlete; I was a natural from watching so many Westerns, and our stunt team helped teach us the rest. It used to drive Paul Baxley crazy that I would pack my punch. (Smacking my fist into the opposite hand before taking a swing.) After, I would shake my hand as if it hurt – because it would be painful if you hit someone in the face. But John Wayne packed his punches and shook his hand, so I did too. If it was good enough for The Duke, it was good enough for *The Dukes*.

I liked taking a punch better than throwing one. My neck was limber, and I had all that bright blond hair to throw around. Wopat's got that stocky football player's build, so he couldn't get the sympathy in a fight like I could. It looks like Tom is beating the crap out of me when we finally step outside to the barn and come to blows in "Carnival of Thrills."

At the end of our fight, my nose is bleeding, and I announce that I'm leaving the farm. Uncle Jesse walks me over to the General as I prepare to go.

"First of all," he says. "I want you to know that I love you dearly." He pulls his handkerchief from his overalls pocket and presses it against my nose. "Blow," Uncle Jesse tells me.

I do and he wipes my nose as he continues. "And second, whenever you get through doin' whatever it is you gotta do, realize that this is your home. You can always come back."

Then he folds the handkerchief and puts it back in his pocket.

Unfortunately, the network thought the handkerchief scene was too much and edited it out. It's a shame, because I thought it was wonderfully played by Denver. When someone truly loves you, they're not worried about getting blood or dirt on their hands. Taking care of your kids comes first.

***

In the early days of *Dukes of Hazzard*, I'd show up on set for call time all sleepy-eyed, and Denver Pyle would already be there, reading the paper with his reading glasses on. We had a routine exchange. "Mornin', John!" Denver would say. "Are you saving your money?"

"No, sir," I'd tell him.

"That's too bad," he'd reply, shaking his head and turning to the next page. "Have you met anybody?"

"Yes, sir, I have."

Then Denver would look over his glasses and ask this: "Does she make you smile?"

If I paused more than a half-second, he'd jump in with, "Well, good luck with that."

A few years later Denver was on cloud nine because he'd met Tippie. "How are you, Denver?" I asked one morning.

"Good on ya," he said. That's what he'd always say.

"Are you saving your money?"

"Yes, I am," he declared.

"Have you met anybody?" I asked.

"Yes, I have," he said, a twinkle in his eye.

I paused, grinning, glad for the opportunity to turn our exchange around. "Does she make you --?"

Before I could finish, Denver replied. "All the time."

I was an eighteen-year-old theater brat when I showed up on *Dukes*, and Denver took me under his wing. He had a strained relationship with his kids, and I believe that during the show, he thought of me as his own son. He had a little office over on Whipple Street in Toluca Lake, and I would visit him there often. Back then, Denver was the only cast member I really had a close relationship with outside of the show. I remember stopping by once when the pace was getting to me. I was burned-out, lonely, and needing to talk. Denver listened, taking it all in, letting me get my story out.

"John, you need a quiet place," Denver said. "Go to the *Irma P.* and think things over a few days." Denver had a houseboat docked over in Marina Del Ray named the *Irma P.* I drove down and spent a long weekend there, thinking about life.

Denver was one of a kind, every bit as wise, kind, and loving as the character he played on Dukes. The night that I am writing this would be his ninety-ninth birthday. I miss Denver. He was my inspiration for Clark Kent's father on *Smallville.* Denver continues to inspire me. I'm thinking about him a lot today and the good things he brought into my life.

***

So how *did* three first cousins end up living with their uncle?

It's a much-discussed part of *Dukes* legend, but it wasn't until years later that Tom, Cathy, and I finally talked it over. We figure our parents were headed out West for the wedding of cousin Sissy Comfurt, traveling through the mountains by train.

"I'll take care of the young-uns," Uncle Jesse assured our folks. "Just drop them kids off at the farm. They can help me with the chores."

The locomotive steamed through the night, the passengers asleep in their coaches, oblivious to the danger that lay ahead. The bridge at Diablo Ridge washed out, collapsed high above the Huerfano River. The steel wheels droned against the track until... silence, as the cars plunged into the cold, dark waters below.

Eighty-seven perished that night in one of the worst train wrecks in U.S. history. Among them, the parents of Lucas, Daisy, and Beauregard Duke.

I like that scenario because it shows Uncle Jesse had to give something up to raise us. Jesse Duke was a widower with no children of his own. I'm not sure that we ever met our Aunt Lavinia. But Jesse still had dreams and choices and a life ahead when he took us in. Uncle Jesse kept his word. He sacrificed his future for our good. He took care of us to his dying day.

The cool thing about *Dukes of Hazzard* is that those answers are left open. The art to making a television show is telling just enough of the story – but not too much. Ultimately, the way Bo, Luke, Daisy, and Uncle Jesse's lives intertwine is up to you, the viewers and fans. You can make up your own story. That way, it becomes your story, too.

***

There was an actors' strike during the filming of season three with members of SAG (Screen Actors Guild) and AFTRA (American Federation of Television and Radio Artists.) Subscription TV services like Showtime and HBO were taking off as LaserDisc and videocassettes started making their way to the general market. Actors didn't feel they were getting a fair share of the new revenue stream, so they went on strike.

Made sense to me. But I didn't have any shows on pay cable or videotape, so I showed up for work the next day. "John, what are you doing here?" The gate guard at Warner Bros. asked.

"Working," I told him.

"You shouldn't be here," he said. "You guys are on strike."

"I don't have a problem with anybody," I replied. "Besides, I've got a call sheet here with my name on it." I held up the sheet to prove it.

"Sorry, John." The guard shook his head. "You can't be here. SAG is on strike."

For the first morning in years, I got to go back to my little two-bedroom condo in the Valley and sleep in.

But not for long. I took on extra work at Celebrity Machines and started negotiations to star in the TV movie *Dream House* with Marilu Henner once the strike was done. My performance of "Still" by the Commodores on the 6th Annual People's Choice Awards had received good reviews earlier that year. Scotti Brothers signed me to a record deal soon after, so I went out on my first concert tour. Acting was off-limits, so I filmed my first music special for CBS called *John Schneider: Back Home.* Back home in Georgia, not New York. The public still believed that I was a born and raised Southern boy. I think I was starting to believe it myself.

But YEE-HAA is more state of mind than geographic location, and I had a bucket-list wish to drive a white Turbo Trans Am through the Boomershine Pontiac showroom window in Decatur and down the streets of Six Flags without getting thrown in jail. So that's exactly what I did. I floored that Firebird down the same theme park streets I once roamed while singing "Sweet Adeline." Not only did I not get arrested, I was cheered on and paid good money. Being on TV is pretty cool sometimes.

My show needed guest stars, and the first person I thought of was Ray Charles. I used to listen to "Born to Lose," "I Got a Woman," and "Lucky Old Sun" in my grandparents' basement with Uncle Butch, and even though the world had passed Ray Charles by for a while, he'd always been one of my favorites. Ray was from Albany, so we sang "Georgia On My Mind" together in an empty theater, and it was a perfect fit for *Back Home.* (Check it out on my YouTube channel.)

Next, the CMA's Entertainer of the Year, Barbara Mandrell, duetted with me on "No. 34 in Atlanta." The song talked about how I'd rather be number thirty-four in Atlanta than number one in L.A. Ironically enough, I was on the number one show in Los Angeles at the time. I loved working in television, but the L.A. attitude never was a good fit for me, then or now. I'd still rather be number thirty-four in Atlanta.

In late October, the actor's strike was settled, and *The Dukes* cast got back to the business of shooting season three. I continued to perform weekend concerts. The air traffic controllers went on strike during the tour, so I drove from show to show, all across America, with my guitar in the passenger seat of my red Maserati. In the spirit of *Smokey and the Bandit* and *Cannonball Run*, I once made it from L.A. to Louisville in twenty-four hours to play the Kentucky State Fair. Crazy.

***

California was so insulated that I could gauge the show's success only when I would head out for weekend shows and special appearances. Thousands of *Dukes* fans began swarming to these events, and I started making more money selling autographed 8 x 10s than I did as a television actor during the week. I would leave a show with a sack literally packed full of five-dollar bills.

The first time I ever saw my picture in a magazine was back in the January '79 issue of *US Weekly*. I happened to be in Palm Springs, so I went every 7-11 in town until I finally found a copy and stared at the postage-stamp sized picture of Bo, Luke, and Daisy with stars in my eyes. A bigger thrill was yet to come. Back then, you knew you'd made it when *Mad* magazine did a parody, and in the December 1980 issue, they ran a piece titled, "The Dopes of Haphazzard." We were good sports about it, even posing for a picture while reading the magazine. Boss holds his nose with one hand and *Mad* in the other while Cletus and Rosco point their pistols at the issue lampooning *The Dukes*.

The *Hazzard* cast eventually swamped the magazine racks, with further parodies by *Cracked* and *Bananas,* a ton of covers for *Tiger Beat, SuperTeen,* and of course, the inevitable gossip about *The Dukes* stars' dating lives in *The National Enquirer.*

I even saw one of my childhood dreams come true. As a boy, I collected issues of *TV Guide*, believing that someday, I'd be in a television show featured inside the weekly magazine. That happened but the dream went one step further. Thirteen-letter word for *Dukes of Hazzard* star? I was one of the answers to the big crossword puzzle in the back of *TV Guide*.

***

Season three's "The Great Santa Claus Chase" is another favorite of mine but in show business, the holiday episodes are usually shot in July. I was burning up in that Santa outfit, wrestling those sticky spruce trees out on scorching, dusty roads. Seems I recall there were six of us dressed like Santa for what seemed like half the show. Me, Tom, and Ben, plus all the bad guys. I believe they put Rick in a Santa suit, too. The writers probably thought it'd be funny to make us sweat.

At the conclusion of the episode, Boss Hogg receives a copy of Dickens'

A Christmas Carol, reads a bit and at least for a moment, sees the light. The Duke family and friends are trimming the tree and singing "Silent Night" when a humble Boss shows up bearing gifts. It's a sweet moment, even if it was mid-summer outside.

The story was a nod to *The Andy Griffith Show* when mean old Ben Weaver has a change of heart and arrives at the jailhouse with presents for the very people he'd been railing against. Christmas should bring out the best, even in the worst of us. It's a time to put aside differences, make peace, and celebrate the things we have in common. Sure, it's idyllic. But in filmmaking, a good redemption story works every time.

We tried to capture that same spirit again in the true-life Duke tribute, *Christmas Cars*. Turn the bad guy good in the blink of an eye and make it believable. That's how change usually happens, in an instant. Who doesn't love a happy ending?

Season Three Squirrels:

- My stunt double, Allan Wyatt Jr., stepped in front of the camera for "Duke Vs. Duke" as Ma Harper's son, "Junior." You'll spot Junior around town in other episodes, sometimes fishing or even delivering pies.

- The General slides up to an antique mirror that supposedly belonged to Robert E. Lee's dentist in the opening of "In this Corner, Luke Duke." Did that stunt myself.

- Jack Gill did season three's famous "barn buster" jump. Jack and I go all the way back to high school. He graduated North Springs and left to be a Hollywood stuntman. I tried to tag along, but Mom said I had to finish school first.

- If you want to see another good Bo thrashing, check out as 6'8" Richard Moll playing "Milo Beaudry" punches me across the Boar's Nest. Richard went on to play the bailiff, "Bull," on *Night Court*.

- I paid tribute to Denver's wise question in my film, *Like Son*. Don Shanks had worked with Denver on *Grizzly Adams,* and they'd shared the same "Does she make you smile?" exchange. Don nails it in the film.

- For the TV movie *Dream House*, I played Charlie Cross, love-struck construction worker from Georgia who moves to New York to build a tiny house for the girl of his dreams. For *Christmas Cars*, talented actor Billy Slaughter plays main character, Charlie Cross.

Holiday Squirrels:

- *Dukes* did give Bo and Luke new shirts once. For Christmas. You'll see us both in green plaid at the end of "The Great Santa Clause Chase."

- I came in to work one day and found a Christmas card addressed to BO HAZZARD COUNTY with a stamp that was drawn on with a crayon. Somehow, it made its way across the country, through Los Angeles and the many divisions of Warner Bros. to my dressing room. I kept that card for years, but like a lot of other treasures, it was lost in the flood. Floods can't take your memories, though. I appreciated the effort some child made to think of me and that the postal workers and studio staff made sure the card found its home. Are you out there, little fella? Bo from Hazzard County's still got an autograph for you.

ANOTHER DAY IN HAZZARD

"Acting is acting. Whether you're doing Hazzard or Hamlet."
— Sorrell Booke

The Dukes of Hazzard was a single-camera show for its entire six-year run. That means for each scene, all of the different shots and angles are done with the same camera. We would shoot a portion of the script from one position, then move the camera, relight the set, and run through it again. Single camera offers more editing choices but requires a lot of technical expertise from the actors to make it look spontaneous while maintaining consistency through multiple takes. (For example, doing the same scene seven times while wearing a Santa outfit in the California sun.)

Dukes was a great show not only due to the cast's connection, but also because of the way it was acted, filmed, and edited together. That's because we learned from legendary actors Denver Pyle, Sorrell Booke, and Jimmie Best. They taught us tricks and details such as this from Sorrell: if you're reading the *Hazzard Gazette* for a wide shot, hold it at arm's length. But if the director's doing a close-up, pull it near your face.

Another great lesson for a restless young man came from Jimmie Best: it's fine to be energetic, but if you move side to side, you're screwed. As an actor, learn to move forward and back. That way, you stay in the shot. However, forward and back can become a focus issue. It's best not to move, but if you have to, as Denver suggested, "Keep your head and shoulders still and wiggle your toes!" The editor's job is to cut all the suck out of a scene, and if you're moving too much, you will get cut. I could deliver the best performance of my life, but if it's not in focus, no one will ever see it.

"Stop watching movies and start watching people, John," Denver would say. He'd done *The Alamo* and many other classic films with John Wayne and said that nobody could be a better friend or worse enemy to an actor than my hero, "The Duke."

Here's one example. When John Wayne worked with actors he liked, he kept his hands low. Actors who were a pain? John Wayne would put his hands high on his hips and stick his elbows out so nobody could stand next to him. He would push that deadbeat actor right out of the frame and force a single shot on himself.

Denver taught us youngsters the old Western method of how to force camera coverage on yourself and ruin a troublemaker's shot. If *The Dukes* cast liked you, we would do everything possible to make sure your scene was great and that you looked good. But if you were difficult, we could also mess up your shot so it wouldn't make the final cut. Fortunately, problem actors on Dukes were few and far between. Because of the demands of our schedule and the difficulties of filming nearly eighty percent of the show outdoors, only old acting pros showed up to play. Then again, that's how they became old pros.

***

Sorrell Booke lived for the challenge of a single-camera show. He was in love with being Boss Hogg and would purposely make the process hard on himself. When you see J.D. light a cigar, reach for a sandwich with his other hand, take a bite, and blow smoke, all while delivering dialogue, understand that Sorrell had to do that sequence exactly the same, each time the camera reset and filmed from another angle.

Sorrell would have to remember when he blew smoke and what word he said before he took a bite from the sandwich in order to perform the scene correctly again. Few comprehend the difficulty of acting at that level, the ability to keep a mental track of every movement while still making it look natural and fun. That's one of my best *Dukes* memories, the sound of Sorrell laughing after he'd pulled off a particularly complicated take.

While Jimmie was more spur-of-the-moment, Sorrell would work out his scenes ahead of time. When he wasn't sitting in his chair doing the *New York Times* crossword puzzle, Sorrell would have his script out, hands moving, figuring out the beats of when to take off his hat and wipe his brow so he could perform consistently for every take. I've had filmmakers thank me for being so easy to edit. Much of that comes from the lessons I learned while watching Sorrell Booke.

Sorrell was short but built like a fireplug, so wardrobe had to rig him up with special padding under his white polyester suit. His face was the only thing close to fat, so he would button his shirt up tight, pull his chin out over the collar and waddle down in it to play the part of Boss.

You'll notice there aren't many scenes exclusively with Bo Duke and Boss Hogg. We finally all meet up at the end of an episode or maybe he's throwing us in jail. Even in those scenes, Boss is with Rosco on one side of the room, while Bo and Luke are on the other, usually figuring out some way to escape.

I hope I'm not ruining the magic, but most of those scenes were shot separately. I wonder if there's much footage out there of Boss Hogg and Bo in the same shot. We were featured in one episode together, "My Son, Bo Hogg." The amnesia storyline was a bit weak, but Don Pedro made his debut as Sheriff Little, and it was fun to play those scenes with Sorrell and call Boss Hogg "Daddy."

Off camera, Sorrell wore big bifocals, and his voice was quieter and more Poindexter-y. He drove an old Volvo sedan to work from the first show in Burbank to the very end. Sorrell also wore the same brown cardigan for all seven seasons, and I don't think he ever washed it.

In real life, Sorrell was not a sloppy person, but his sweater had food stains all over it. I have a feeling Sorrell was superstitious, and the brown cardigan was part of his "getting ready to become Boss Hogg" outfit. Jimmie Best used to give him grief about that sweater, and Sorrell would just smile and keep his mouth shut. He would never let you in on his secrets.

We were celebrating the end of season three at Sorrell's house in nearby Sherman Oaks, and the cast was sitting around a big table on his back porch playing Indian Poker. That's the game where you lick the back of a card, stick it on your forehead, and you can see everyone's card but your own. You up the ante based on the cards that are visible and how the other players bet.

Sorrell won every single hand. There were eight of us, and I guess he had the mathematical skill to look at the cards that were showing, figure out the statistical odds, and wager accordingly. Sorrell had a degree from Columbia, a master of fine arts from Yale; he spoke five languages and served as a counterintelligence officer in the Korean War. Still, we accused him of cheating that night on his porch! We had a lot of laughs together, but sadly, that was the only time I ever spent with Sorrell Booke away from *The Dukes* set.

***

We filmed *Dukes of Hazzard* by set locations rather than by any sort of sequence to the story. Every scene in the episode that takes place outside the farmhouse would be filmed at the same time. Let's say Bo and Luke drive up in the General, get out, and run through the kitchen door for the show's opening. After the first commercial break, Uncle Jesse gets a call on the CB while sharpening his axe by the trough. At the end of the episode, the Duke family stands on the porch steps waving goodbye to Enos. We would shoot all three of those scenes back to back while everyone was on location at the farmhouse.

After that, we would pack up and shoot every scene that took place outside of the Boar's Nest. Then to the Hazzard County Courthouse and so on. Once the exterior scenes were done, we'd start on the interior ones at Warner Stage 28 and 28A. (We had two soundstages full of sets, which later became home to NBC's hit, *The West Wing*.) In some shots, you can see a WB soundstage behind Cooter's, like the scene at Boss's Caddy near the end of "In this Corner, Luke Duke." It's a giant building with a round roof, kind of like a Quonset hut. I hear they've since painted that soundstage sky blue with puffy clouds in an effort to camouflage it a little. Movie tricks!

The Dukes of Hazzard was a rural show, so we didn't have all that many indoor sets. The rooms of the farmhouse were located on Stage 28A, and the Dukes' kitchen and living room were together in one big set. Warner built Bo and Luke's bedroom once, best I can recall, and I think they used a generic one for the occasional scene in Daisy's room.

All the interior walls in Hazzard County would fly. The farmhouse, police station, Boss Hogg's house, the Boar's Nest. If the director decided to shoot from a certain angle, the crew would unbolt the wall and get rid of it. So rather than move me to the other end of the couch, they would move the wall. I never quite did understand the logic of portable walls.

At the sheriff's station, the stairs to the basement jail didn't actually go anywhere. We would walk down three steps and then have to squat and fake it after that. The set for the basement cells was in a different area of

Stage 28, and those stairs led up to a dead end as well.

You'll notice we rarely looked toward the back wall of the Boar's Nest – because there wasn't one. That's where the camera and film gear were located. By the way, beer served at the Boar's Nest was real and so was the pinball machine. In a tip of the hat to Rosco, it was a 1975 table called *Sheriff*. The producers must have figured out I was a pinball fan because they kept it lit up but silent and out of operation. Tom and I were so competitive, it could've put us behind schedule for sure.

The most difficult scenes to shoot were those final segments where we've chased down the bad guys, and *The Dukes* cast is gathered around the cars. Because it required the entire ensemble, those scenes were usually shot around lunch, which was high noon and the hottest, most miserable time of the day. The sun would be directly overhead, so the crew would have to pump in a ton of light to combat the shadows.

I was a blond-haired, blue-eyed guy standing in a dirt intersection over a white cop car with an army of hot lights beaming down on me. The temperature was about a hundred and ten degrees, and it was so bright under the lights that I could barely see my co-stars. But my job was to smile, laugh, and make it all look easy, like just another day in Hazzard.

***

From the fourth season on, we started having a "process day" where we shot nothing but scenes in the car. The General Lee Tom and I used on process day had no engine or wheels. One crew member could move it with a dolly, and we would film every scene with the General from that episode using rear-screen video projection behind us with footage of country roads shot by the second unit to match the stunts.

For process day, we usually had our scripts sitting on the car seat so we could run through scenes from start to finish of the show. We learned several little tricks to simulate driving through the country in those days. There was an apple box sitting at the front of the engine-less General, and one crew member's job was to take a two-by-four and rock the car side to side to give it some movement. Another guy would spray Fuller's earth into an effects fan to mimic kicking up dust on a dirt road. A third guy had a 650-watt "tweenie" light on a high stand so he could simulate the movement of the sun as we drove through the countryside. As cheesy as those parts of the show might look sometimes, there was a lot going on behind the scenes to make it feel authentic.

Tom and I spent a lot of time singing in the General between takes. Creedence Clearwater's "Lookin' Out My Back Door" and "Up on Cripple Creek" by The Band. The Eagles, "Take it Easy" and *Hee Haw*'s theme, "Pfft, You Were Gone."

There should be hours of footage of me and Tom harmonizing, but back then, once the director got what he wanted, he'd circle the print, and the studio would process only those parts. In the digital world, everything you shoot exists. With film, you kept only the director's picks. The remaining film would then get re-silvered and used again. A few singing scenes made it on the show ("A Baby for the Dukes") but we were both pursuing careers in music and felt it was best to keep the two worlds separate.

Tom and I drank a good bit of beer while waiting in the General, too. We called it a "snapper." Bill Belt was our prop guy, and we'd shoot him a look and mimic popping the top off a can. Bill would nod back and say, "Two Vernors, coming right up!"

Vernors was a popular ginger ale in the early '80s, but that wasn't what we were drinking. Bill would fill our red Solo cups with Coors. We never got drunk, though. It was hot in Southern California, and back then, there was no bottled water to speak of. So, we'd cool off with a few snappers between takes and sing our favorite songs.

Those are some of my favorite memories on *Dukes*, sitting in that shell of a car with Tom, drinking a cold beer, singing Eagles songs. Good times.

***

One morning during the filming of season four, Tom rolled his tan Alfa Romeo Spider down the switchback curves of Topanga Canyon Road. Nobody wore seat belts back then, but the Spider was a tiny two-seater convertible, not some giant land boat. Good thing Tom was farm-tough, as he held himself in by the steering wheel as the Alfa tumbled into a ditch, narrowly escaping a drop down the steep hills of Encino.

Somewhere in the crash, Tom cracked his head open and had to go to the emergency room so they could stitch up the gash. He still showed up on set, ready to work. There was no stopping Tom Wopat. Like me, he was a theater brat. Rain, shine, drunk, sober, healthy, or sick – the show must go on. (Tom banged the dents out of his Alfa and still has it to this day.)

I wish I could remember what episode we were shooting that week. He had his accident on process day, so we had to reconfigure things so the camera could shoot from Tom's left side. I recall one scene where we're motoring along in the General, and I'm spouting off about how unfair our situation is, how the system is crooked, and I think we should fight back.

"Just keep drivin', Bo," Luke growls, not even turning to look at me. He couldn't turn. The right side of his face was so stitched-up and swollen that he looked like an alien.

***

I wrecked the General Lee only once.

Tom and I were driving down Maverick Street at the Warner backlot on our way to lunch, and I was teaching him how to throw a 90. "Okay, you gotta use the emergency brake," I said, "And when you get just shy of ninety degrees, lock up all four brakes, and the car will slide sideways."

Tom nodded, but you can't simply tell someone how to do a 90-degree slide. You have to show them. Maverick Street was a dirt road in the Old West area of the studio and made a sharp curve right. "Okay, watch," I told Tom. "I'll slide up right next to that building."

I gunned it and cut the Charger's wheel. Then I hit the brake. Late. If you don't hit all four brakes before 90, the rear end will continue to slide.

I can still hear the narration in Waylon's voice. *...and that's how Hazzard County's General Lee crashed into Walnut Grove's Harriet Olsen School for the Blind. You reckon they'll call Cooter? Or Pa Ingalls' mule?*

I had to report to the captain of Warner's Transportation Department and tell him I'd wrecked a brand-new General Lee picture car. The one with the fancy chrome-plated springs under the hood. But before long, Tom and I were back on the road again in another General. It was good to be Bo!

"Okay, so how 'bout the 180?" Tom asked.

"Well," I replied, pushing the accelerator to the floor. "For the 180, keep your foot on the emergency brake. As it swings around, transfer over to the gas...."

As Tom improved, our competitive nature took over, and we'd try to slide the General without spilling the other's coffee. I got smooth enough to where I could throw a 90 and never spill a drop from Tom's cup. (Probably because I'd come in at night and practice.) Poor Tom. He'd usually end up running into something. Bo's yellow shirt got a lot of coffee stains on it.

And God forbid if Cathy was driving. But that's a story for another day.

***

The Bo Duke in the pilot was the same as the one in the series finale and in every season between. Luke, Daisy, and Uncle Jesse? They stayed the same. I believe that you can destroy a show with character development. To me, a successful TV show is the same people in different situations. *I Love Lucy*, *The Andy Griffith Show*, *The Simpsons*. There's little, if any character development as the series progresses. Bo Duke didn't need to grow or become more analytical. The comfort of *Dukes of Hazzard* was in its familiarity.

Of course, we can't take credit because that's the way our characters were written, and I'd be lying if I didn't say that at the time we filmed those shows, it often felt like the scripts were becoming a little flat. Luke is hypnotized. Bo gets amnesia. Boss has a twin brother who is exactly his opposite. We were working through all the same old sitcom clichés.

I complained about the storylines back then just like everybody else. What ridiculous thing would kick off this week's episode? Bo and Luke find a million dollars in the creek? ("The Great Hazzard Hijack.") A Bugs Bunny doll full of diamonds falls out of the sky? ("Diamonds in the Rough.") What's next? A General Lee chase scene with Wile E. Coyote? Robots? Aliens? (Just wait.)

Shows like *M.A.S.H.* and *Friends* would occasionally replace the writers. Give them a nice severance and bring in a fresh group to write new shows. *Dukes of Hazzard* never did that. The series was a hit, and our writers were getting great paychecks, but I don't think they bragged at cocktail parties about working on *Dukes*. Nobody seemed proud of the series but us. Even though we were a number-one show, we were still seen as the red-headed stepchild of CBS. It seemed like the network didn't care regardless of how well we did in the ratings.

Hell, I don't get it, the studio execs would say. *But it's paying the bills, and I just built a swimming pool, so God bless The Dukes.*

That's another reason our cast and crew became so tight. We had to work as a team, not only to meet a tough schedule but also to help each other look good and try to make the show better. The network's lack of support brought us closer and made us that much more determined to succeed. In difficult times, one of us would raise our fist and proclaim, "WE ARE . . ."

The rest would join in and rally like a football team, "...THE DUKES!"

Season Four Squirrels:

- Scotti Brothers released *The Dukes of Hazzard* soundtrack in spring 1982. Boss Hogg was the narrator; Johnny Cash cut a great song called "The General Lee," and I contributed two numbers, "In the Driver's Seat" and for the expanded CD, "Them Good Ol' Boys Are Bad." My favorite cut is Rosco's ode to his sidekick, "Flash." Jimmie was Flash's real-life owner, and it was his idea to bring a basset hound to the Hazzard police force.

- Some observant *Dukes* fans think those are my hands doubling Boss Hogg for the card deal in "Ten Million Dollar Sheriff," but it was actually Jeff Altman, who played Hughie Hogg. I was good at card tricks, but Jeff was a master. Those are my hands shuffling the deck for Denver in "Route 7-11."

- Another tale of Wopat's stubborn work ethic: Tom showed up one morning in a strange vehicle. He got out, tapped the roof and offered an exhausted, "Thanks." Turns out he'd been working in Vegas, and his car had been stolen. Tom had to hitchhike through the desert all night, but he was there at Disney Ranch, ready to work at six a.m. There were no cell phones in those days, so you had to figure it out. We did whatever we had to do to keep *The Dukes* moving on down the road. -

- Over the years, some have suggested that you can't squeal tires on a dirt road. Sorry, skeptics, but if it's hard-packed dirt that's been there since the Civil War or silent movies – yes, you can. I did it many times in the Boar's Nest parking lot. Speaking of redneck magic, when the stunt team wanted a little spin and smoke, they would spray the wheels with a mixture of WD-40 and Clorox. Only for the underpowered cars.

- In late '82, I played author Nick Callohan in a romantic comedy called *Happy Endings* for Motown Productions. It was nominated for a Primetime Emmy and was the first television movie produced by Suzanne DePasse.

- Warner called it Maverick Street because they filmed the Jim Garner Western *Maverick* there. It was also the town set just outside of Fort Courage in one of my favorite shows, *F Troop*. No matter how successful *Dukes* became, I was always honored to be welcomed on such hallowed, Hollywood ground.

- A poll was conducted asking which public figure schoolkids would most like to meet. In first place, President Ronald Reagan. Second? Bo Duke.

THE HAZARDS OF DUKES:
COY, VANCE & THE TROUBLE WITH SEASON FIVE

*"Sometimes if you want to see a change for the better,
you have to take things into your own hands."*
– Clint Eastwood

The Dukes of Hazzard toys first appeared in the 1981 Mego Catalog, and merchandise kicked in like crazy after that, even beating *Star Wars* in sales for that year. It was strange seeing my face on beach towels, Underoos and especially that freaky-looking mask that was part of the Bo Duke Halloween costume. Having my own action figure was cool, though, so I didn't give the financial end much thought at first.

The product line expanded, and pretty soon the Duke name was plastered on everything, including Big Wheels, satin jackets, blue jeans, nightgowns, cowboy hats, record players, playing cards, pinball machines, walkie-talkies, yo-yos, coloring books, calendars, and guitars. The Montgomery Ward Christmas catalog featured four whole glossy pages devoted solely to *Dukes of Hazzard* merchandise.

The most popular item was the Barnbusters play set, which was a wind-up "Super General Lee Stunt Charger" that kids could crash through a plastic barn. Warner Bros. didn't put our photo on the box for the Barnbusters set or several other best-selling *Dukes* items, but my mom (who was also president of my fan club) would go to the stores and take snapshots of the displays. More often than not, they had cardboard stand-ups of me, Tom, and Cathy set up to promote the toys. The new influx of cash didn't seem to be reaching our pockets, so we brought this to the studio's attention. (For the record, I am not speaking for Tom here. We're best buddies, but it's not my place to say how he felt during this time.)

Turns out, there was a pretty severe oversight in the accounting that wasn't exactly in our favor, so we felt we had no choice but to sue for damages. If we won, we agreed to share proceeds with the March of Dimes and a relief fund for the families of eight coal miners killed in Topmost, Kentucky. I despise lawsuits but thought for sure that would get the studio's attention, and the situation would be resolved. It wasn't. They didn't even reply.

We refused to return to the set of *Dukes* until the matter was settled. The battle turned ugly as Warner Bros. countersued, postponed filming, and announced an open cattle call for actors to replace Bo and Luke.

I told the producers if they were looking for a new Bo Duke, there was a guy I knew from Atlanta named Byron Cherry who'd be perfect for the role. We'd done some soft drink commercials together back when I was a teen, and we looked enough alike that casting directors would occasionally try to cast us as brothers.

The studio still considered over two thousand actors before finally bringing in Chris Mayer and... Byron Cherry. Byron was my buddy, and I had no hard feelings toward him for taking the part. I picked him up at the airport, let him stay in my condo, and even gave him my lucky brass and abalone belt buckle for his screen test.

"Don't make any long-term plans for this part," I told Byron. "I don't think it will last." I believed the matter would be settled quickly, fairly, and the studio would call us back in at any moment.

I was still across the street from Warner Bros. at Celebrity Machines, selling Porsches and working on stars' Ferraris. One day, a CBS business executive brought his Jag in for repair. (Remember, Warner produced the show for CBS.) He pulled me to the side and said, "This will not go well for you, John."

"How could it not?" I asked. "We're right. We know exactly what happened."

"Trust me," he said. "The studio will cancel the series first."

In the meantime, the show had sunk from consistent top-ten ratings to low fifties and falling. Apparently, Hazzard didn't feel right with someone else at the wheel of the General. Insulted by the change, viewers revolted, and advertisers were following their lead.

Tom and I met with Warner Bros. in late November, and both sides agreed to drop the lawsuits and move on. The studio made an official announcement right before Christmas, and we returned to *Dukes* in a canary yellow Mustang for season five's nineteenth episode.

"Welcome Back, Bo 'N' Luke" had to be difficult for Byron and Chris. I've heard there were plans for a special episode featuring all four Duke boys teaming up against an especially despicable threat to Hazzard, but in the end, we shot a quick scene in the farmhouse living room pairing me and Chris on one couch with Tom and Byron on the other.

With a quick explanation to Daisy, Uncle Jesse, and *Dukes* viewers (Aunt Bessie is ill/Bo and Luke got homesick), we headed outside, and they handed back the keys to the General Lee. We shook hands, hugged necks, and as their Mustang drives away, Luke shakes his head and says, "What a pair." At that moment, Byron Cherry was off camera, dropping his pants and showing us his shiny white Georgia moon.

And just like that, Coy and Vance were never seen again.

***

About the only thing we accomplished in our absence was getting Sonny Shroyer back on the show. Sonny had left to do a spinoff called *Enos* where he stars as a country detective transferred to the LAPD. (Think *Beverly Hillbillies* meets *McCloud*.) *Enos* was written by Gy Waldron and produced by Warner, but for some reason didn't catch on with viewers and was cancelled after only one season.

Warner Bros. left Sonny hanging, and we wanted him back on *Dukes*. Mike Gursey was both my and Sonny's manager at the time, and with a whole lot of help from him, Enos came home from Los Angeles and back into his Hazzard patrol car. Rick Hurst got to stay as well, which I thought was great because "Cletus" was always a joy to work with.

I told a Sonny story already, so here's one on Rick: We were shooting "Road Pirates," and Bo and Luke are making an escape from jail with Deputy Cletus Hogg handcuffed in-between. We bound down the Hazzard County Courthouse steps, split two different directions at the curb and accidently run Cletus into a light post.

When Rick hit the pole, the antique globe fell from the top, smashed me in the head, bounced off the squad car's light bar, and somehow landed in my hands. They're made of plastic now, but back then the fixtures were solid glass and weighed about fifteen pounds. For a moment, I was dazed.

The director stopped filming, and Rick grabbed on to me because he was so concerned that I'd been hurt. Miraculously, neither my skull or the glass had cracked, so we backed up and did the scene again. For that shot, we pulled in tighter and left the glass on Hazzard's sidewalk.

It's ironic that Rick played Boss's cousin, because in many ways, he and Sorrell really were alike. Rick had degrees in psychology and theater from Tulane and a master of fine arts in acting from Temple University. He was a meticulous actor, and like Sorrell, put a lot of thought into his character, even the parts that seemed ridiculous. Rick wanted Cletus to have his own version of Enos's "Possum on a gum bush!" and finally came up with "Buzzards on a buzz saw!" and "Flapjacks on a Ferris wheel!" We thought his play on words was brilliant and silly, both.

Sorrell was not afraid to do the physical comedy that *Dukes* demanded, and neither was Rick. In the previous scene from "Road Pirates," Sorrell takes a dive into wet cement on the courthouse steps. (Waylon: "Boss's paving company mixes the only cement thin enough to fish in.") The next thing you see is a handcuffed Cletus running headfirst into a light pole. Watch how much the post shimmies when he hits it. Rick was nearly 6'5" in his boots, and for a tall, heavyset guy, could pull off a terrific pratfall, heels over his head, arms in the air, landing flat on his back in the street.

With great tenacity and little success, Rick has also been the one to take on Warner Bros. concerning unpaid royalties on *Dukes* merchandise over the years – not only for himself, but for the entire cast even Coy and Vance.

Sadly, Chris "Vance Duke" Mayer passed away in 2011. Anything gained for him from Rick's efforts will go to his family.

***

Ultimately, Warner Bros. was just doing their job back then, which was to stick to the accounting method they had in place for merchandising rights. No one expected a line of *Dukes* merch to beat *Star Wars*. Not the studio, nor the actors. I shouldn't have taken it so personally.

I didn't work for eighteen episodes, which I needed in order to pay income tax for the previous year. The money you make to pay back taxes?

Well, you owe tax on that money too. It's easy to get behind, and that's where my troubles with the IRS began.

In hindsight, it was a blessing that we dropped the suits and returned to *Dukes of Hazzard*. If I'd have won that lawsuit against Warner Bros., no studio would have touched me with a thousand-foot pole. It's likely that I would have never worked in Hollywood again. (Certainly not for the WB. It'd break my heart to see someone else play *Smallville's* Jonathan Kent.)

I've seen only one episode from the Coy and Vance era, and it wasn't until years later. I can see where some fans say it feels a bit forced. Byron Cherry didn't have to act country; he *was* country. If Warner Bros. would have let Byron be himself, they might have never asked me to come back to the show.

Chris and Byron jumped in and did the best they could in an impossible situation with unreasonable expectations and dialogue that had been written for Bo and Luke. Tom and I knew the dialogue was weak, so we'd improvise to make things conversational, whereas the new Duke boys were expected to stick to the words as written.

There was something unusually authentic about Bo and Luke rambling around Hazzard County. They really do come off like a couple of good ol' boys making their way, the only way they know how. Even now, I watch *Dukes* and think, *by God, this feels like it's actually happening. Like it's real.*

***

KABC news anchor and former Miss America, Tawny Little, came to interview me at Celebrity Machines about the Bo and Luke strike. I took her for a ride down Buena Vista in my '66 Corvette, and we hit it off. She was L.A.'s number-one newscaster, and I was their number-one redneck. We were quite an unlikely pair.

Tawny and I got married under the Hazzard gazebo in the summer of 1983. Our crew fixed up the set like a *Dukes* wedding episode, and in my Aston Martin Vantage, I arrived for the ceremony wearing a white linen suit with a red vest and Colonel Sanders-style ribbon tie.

My family and fellow cast members attended along with a few hundred other guests, dining at tables set out in the street by Boss Hogg's house. Sorrell pretended to be disappointed that he wasn't asked to officiate, and some made cracks that maybe the General Lee should've been my best man. When the judge asked Tawny if she took me, John Richard Schneider, in marriage, she smiled and said, "You betcha."

Then we jumped on a helicopter to the Virgin Islands for a much-needed break from TV.

Season Five Squirrel Nest:

- In early 1983, Warner Bros. partnered with *Jetsons* and *Scooby-Doo* producer Hanna-Barbera to create *The Dukes* Saturday morning cartoon. Byron and Chris voiced the characters for the first season, and we took over for season two. The General Lee flew; the Duke family traveled to Ireland, Austria, and the Philippines, and some say the storylines were better than its live-action counterpart. It took two days to record voiceovers for each episode, and I'm still not sure where we found the time. As a kid, I loved cartoons. Still do.

- *Dukes* often had visitors to the set, and we always stopped to spend time with them, especially the kids, who frequently had special needs. It was heartbreaking, but you had to be strong because that child was looking to you as a source of strength and inspiration. I wanted to figure out a way to do more, and it's one of the things that drove me to help start the Children's Miracle Network.

- Remember Steve Hanks who auditioned with me for the part of Bo? Steve returned to *Dukes* as crop duster pilot and Daisy's beau, Darcy Kincaid, for season five's "Daisy's Shotgun Wedding."

- Jimmie Best had another fallout with the producers and vowed to "do the dialogue as written" if they didn't correct an issue on how Flash's trainer, Alvin Mears, was paid. Warner Bros. refused, so Jimmie stopped ad-libbing for an episode. Wish I could remember which one. If you see Rosco being unusually stiff, that's it. The situation with Alvin was corrected quickly.

- Gary Baxley followed in his Uncle Paul's footsteps by becoming second-unit director and stunt coordinator for *Enos*. He also coordinated the stunts I did for a movie with Kirk Douglas called *Eddie Macon's Run*.

• Actually, you can see "Coy Duke" again. Byron and I remain friends, and he makes a special appearance in *Christmas Cars*. Viewers will finally discover what Coy has been up to since he roared away from the farm in that yellow Mustang. Fans still tell me, "Coy just never could drive that car like you, Bo!" That's hilarious because it was the exact same stunt crew behind the wheel. Byron and I talk about that in *Christmas Cars* too.

NOW LEAVING HAZZARD COUNTY

"People are always looking for the easy way out.
God help me, I hope I never find the easy way. I like a good struggle."
— Vince Gironda

The last two seasons of *Dukes* were a blur. Sometimes it was hard to tell one episode from another. Outsiders showed up to pull various kidnapping and robbery schemes. More trouble at the Hazzard County Orphanage. Luke's long-lost brother shows up this time, and now Daisy is the one who gets hypnotized. Rosco has an evil twin. Boss discovers a genie in a lamp. We were going through the motions by then.

There were a few bright spots. After a hundred and thirty-one episodes of narration and guitar-picking, we finally showed The Balladeer's face in "Welcome, Waylon Jennings," and for "Go West, Young Dukes," the show traveled back to 1880s-era Hazzard so the Duke gang (our ancestors Joe and Hank Duke, that is) could take on Frank and Jesse James. I got to live out my dream and go full-on Western, complete with ten-gallon hat, bullwhip, long duster, low-slung six-shooter, horse, handlebar mustache, and even a good old-fashioned fistfight in the local saloon.

Then again, there was "Robot P. Coltrane" and "Strange Visitor to Hazzard," which included a rare scene of the General driving at night. Fonzie jumped a shark; Bobby Ewing returned from the dead, and the final season of *Dukes of Hazzard* featured a four-foot tall green alien that Bo and Luke affectionately refer to as "little cousin."

Sorrell Booke directed the episode (which decades later is a lot of fun) and stuntman/former Ewok, Felix Silla, guest-starred as our extraterrestrial visitor in a cheap-looking rubber suit. Oddly enough, Silla's most well-known role was as a famous little cousin. He played Cousin Itt on the '60s TV series, *The Addams Family*.

Season seven also included "Happy Birthday, General Lee," a flashback episode explaining how a black Dodge Charger from the Capitol City wrecking yard became an official member of the Duke family with a roll bar, welded-shut doors, and 01 on the sides. As for the color of the world's most famous car? "This all the paint you got here, Cooter?" Uncle Jesse asks, looking over a few cans on the garage shelf.

"I'm a little thin in the paint department," Cooter replies. "But that's a real nice reddish-orange."

Unfortunately, the tribute episode begins with a miniature General Lee jumping through a moving drainpipe. Ouch.

Switching to the use of miniatures for the car stunts was a morale killer on the *Hazzard* set. Paul Baxley quit, and the greatest stunt team on television suddenly had nothing to do except take jobs with newer thrill-filled shows like *The A-Team, Knight Rider,* and *The Fall Guy.*

Producers made the change to save money, not realizing that tiny cars also meant tiny roads, trees, telephone poles, railroad tracks, and trains. The construction of miniature sets ended up costing more than the original stunts.

The General Lee was a star in his own right, receiving as many as thirty thousand fan letters a month. And that wasn't just NASCAR fans in south Alabama. *The Dukes of Hazzard* was a ratings smash from BBC1 in the United Kingdom to Italy's Canale 5. It was a slap in the face to change our signature car jumps to cheesy miniatures that looked so fake on TV.

Fans still love to talk about those classic General Lee jumps. You can feel the brutality of the impact, see the fenders buckling, and hear the shocks groan. There's movement and action and a sexy kind of violence to those scenes. The biggest difference is that, before miniatures, we never did anything that couldn't actually be done in a car. (Except for driving away from a frame-crushing jump, that is.)

The miniature General Lee was actually about two feet long, and had blacked-out windows, and it would bounce through the shots in a way that was more cartoonish than anything close to natural. Since they weren't limited by danger, gravity, or stunt drivers, the writing team started coming up with scenes that made the General fly in ways that were completely preposterous. We would leap through culverts being moved by cranes, bunny hop over grain silos and two-story houses. I'd go do some car show in Minnesota, and fans would say, "We saw you jump through the culvert the other night!"

Thank God the General's windows were blacked out, or they would've had to put a miniature Bo Duke inside, hiding his face in shame.

***

It was just after *Dukes* had moved to Burbank, and I was on set doing ADR, which stands for Automated Dialogue Replacement. ADR is the process where you go back and re-record your lines to make small changes or improve the quality of the sound. Sometimes the car might drown out part of your dialogue, or the producer makes adjustments to the script after the scenes were shot.

While I was working, a tour bus pulled up with a few motorcycles riding shotgun. A bunch of rough characters started milling about. The bus door opened, and the roughest, meanest-looking one climbed out and walked over to me, a beautiful lady with piercing blue eyes standing by his side. It was Waylon and Jessi Colter.

Long hair, black hat, leather vest, cigarette between his teeth. Waylon looked like he'd been up for days. "Yes, sir, hello!" I said, excited and standing to shake his hand. "So nice to meet you."

"Hang on a second, Hoss," said Waylon. He got out his wallet and started digging through it, guitar picks and twenty-dollar bills, crumpled uncashed checks. Finally, he pulled out a piece of wadded-up paper. "Lil feller handed this to me at a concert couple weeks ago and asked if I'd give it to Bo," Waylon said. "So here you go."

He placed the scrap of paper in my outstretched hand. I unfolded it. After two weeks in Waylon's wallet, the letters were a smudged mess, and it smelled like sweat and Marlboro smoke. But here he was, hell-raising rebel and adopted son of Hells Angels, carrying around a note some little kid gave him and making sure that he did what he promised to do. That was a pretty cool way to meet Waylon Jennings.

He'd stopped by *The Dukes* set to film his part for the show's intro. We were shooting at a junkyard out in the San Fernando Valley, and the crew put up a black tarp so they could get some footage of Waylon playing his famous '53 leather-bound Telecaster. Before, *Dukes* was using a generic shot of a guy in a blue shirt (not Tom or me) strumming an acoustic guitar.

Waylon would visit the set occasionally, but our paths didn't cross much until he came back to guest-star in the final season. I was married to Tawny then, and we had Waylon and Jessi over for dinner one night. I'd heard he loved ribs and guaranteed him that ours were the best in town.

Tawny was the top news anchor in Los Angeles back then. She didn't know how to cook ribs, nor did she have the time, so I ran down to a rib joint in Burbank, bought a rack, and pretended that we made them ourselves. Waylon said they were delicious, but he was probably being nice. Everybody knew ribs were Waylon's favorite, so that's probably what he got every time someone invited him over. I can just imagine him pulling hard on that Marlboro and saying, "Damn, Jessi. Ribs again."

Waylon had a rough reputation – and deserved it – but he was thoughtful and caring down deep. He hated the business and the bankers and always stood up for blue-collar workers and the common man, for children and old folks, for the underprivileged and those struggling just to get by. When most people hear *The Dukes of Hazzard* theme they think of Bo and Luke, but that's Waylon's song, too. He was a true outlaw, the real deal, what country singers nowadays can only pretend to be. Fighting the system, making trouble by avoiding it, never meaning no harm. Waylon Jennings was the original "Good Ol' Boy."

***

It's a myth that *Dukes* scripted shirtless scenes for Bo and Luke to lure in female viewers. Tom and I took our shirts off because we were supposed to be chopping wood in the South. Do country boys wear shirts while doing farm chores? Of course not.

Tom was built like a brick outhouse, like the cornfed dairy farmer that he was. We used to call him "the coat hanger" because his traps started at his earlobes, and he was so lean that you could see every muscle rippling as he swung the axe. (Decades later, Tom's still ripped.)

The best shape I was ever in during *Dukes* was for season seven's, "Cool Hands, Luke and Bo." That's the one where the Duke boys are arrested on trumped-up traffic charges and sentenced to the Osage County chain gang. Morgan Woodward had played a cruel, mirrored sunglasses-wearing chain boss in the Paul Newman classic *Cool Hand Luke* and reprised that character for our episode. "Takin' it off, sir!" That was our line to the prison guards when we'd pull our shirts off, which was pretty frequent in this episode.

I'd been working out diligently at Vince's Gym on Ventura Blvd. Vince Gironda was known as the "Iron Guru" and had a reputation for being notoriously harsh. The movie studios would send actors over for Vince to whip into shape, but I had signed up on my own when I first moved to L.A.

Cher, Robert Blake, Michael Landon, Kurt Russell, Burt Reynolds, Carl Weathers – they were all around back then. Arnold Schwarzenegger and Lou Ferrigno from *The Hulk* worked out at Vince's as well. David Lee Roth was there with us, and Vince used to give him hell about his flamboyant outfits. Dave trained hard, though, and looks like a million bucks in those old Van Halen videos.

Vince didn't care if you were the biggest star on the planet; he had no patience for screwing around. Fortunately, he seemed to like me and always went the extra mile to help out, often pairing me with WWF wrestler "Rowdy" Roddy Piper for workouts. Once, Piper was getting ready for what I believe is John Carpenter's best film, *They Live*. We'd been through the gauntlet when Vince looked Roddy over and pointed to the row machine. "Ok, Hot Rod, gimme seventy-five reps."

We were spent. I couldn't have done one rep, much less seventy-five. For a quick moment, Roddy looked defeated. Then, he got this look on his face like a rabid dog. He grabbed the bar and rowed like a madman until he finished every last rep. It was a lesson to me on pushing past your limits.

I'd let Vince know if I had a scene coming up where I needed to take my shirt off. "All right, kid," he'd say. "How much time ya got?"

"Two weeks from Thursday, Vince."

Vince would pepper his speech with a few choice adjectives before putting me on a grueling workout and Spartan diet. "Nothing but meat and water ten days before the shoot. Any kinda meat you want, any kind of water."

The proof of Vince's methods is in "Cool Hands, Luke and Bo." The great thing about that episode is that we were rescued by none other than Boss and Rosco. Even if we had to turn around and rescue them again. Fans love those rare occasions where Boss and the Duke boys team up, and so did we.

Vince Gironda taught me that exercise doesn't have to complicated. Master the basics; make them your own, and find creativity within those limits. Complex is rarely better; it usually just complicates things. At the time, I thought Vince was teaching me about fitness, but turns out, those values were universal.

Losing fifty pounds at age fifteen was a turning point for me, but a few years ago, life got crazy, and I let my weight creep up again. When you're overweight, your body is just trying to survive. It's hard to function when you're in a fog, and I found myself having to go back to those same basic principles again. Exercise is not about bulging biceps or six-pack abs. It's about living life to the fullest. Commitment to health and fitness changes the way you work, rest, play, your relationship with God and family and friends.

I was up past one a.m. working on this book but set the alarm for six-thirty so I could get in a round of P-90X with a workout partner. Much younger guy, super-lean. Smoked him, though. Left him in the dust. Fear motivates me. In my mind, I'm still that overweight kid. And I don't ever want to go back there again.

***

I got the opportunity to write and direct what would turn out to be our final episode, "Opening Night at the Boar's Nest." Ever since I was a kid shooting my own Super 8 films, I had dreams of directing, and the process gave me a new appreciation for what the writers and crew went through. I still have the thick green leather script binder with my original production notes, including a ton of sketches I did on camera angles and shots. I worked around the clock on that episode, but it was important to prove that I could do the job.

For "Lulu's Hogg's Big Charity Talent Show" at the Boar's Nest, The Duke Family Singers harmonized on Tom T. Hall's "Fox on the Run," Sorrell wore a pink tutu, and "Coltrano the Great" made Boss disappear.

At that point in the series, I thought it was important to show the relationship between Rosco and Boss Hogg. Jimmie was an amazing actor, and I wanted to give him a chance to show his chops. It's a special moment in Hazzard history when he's sitting in a dim-lit Boar's Nest, surrounded by candles, crying and trying to get his little fat buddy back.

Boss catches sight of him through the window, and for once, isn't concerned about his pocketbook. J.D. Hogg might have been a greedy cuss, but Sorrell Booke was a kind and compassionate man. I'm glad that in those final minutes we were able to let a little more of Sorrell shine through Boss Hogg.

Dukes fans often ask why the show didn't go out with more of a bang, one last special episode that saw Uncle Jesse pay off the farm or at least let Bo and Luke off probation. Truth is, the network still wasn't in our corner, at least not enough to give us a proper goodbye. We'd heard rumors that the series would be ending after season seven, but I don't think I believed it back then. We were still a top-twenty show, and I felt certain a last-minute call would come saying there couldn't be a world without *The Dukes*. For the record, the show was never officially cancelled. CBS just didn't pick us up for season eight.

Entertainment Tonight came out to film a special farewell segment to *The Dukes of Hazzard*. The cast gathered on stage at the Boar's Nest for our final scene, and as director of the episode, I said, "Cut! Ladies and gentlemen, that is a wrap. A seven-year wrap. We are done, finished. *Dukes* is over. We love you."

And that's how the show ended. With Me, Tom, Cathy, Denver, Sorrell, Ben, Sonny, and Jimmie together in one last embrace. In some sense, just the way we'd started. It's as good an ending as any.

And don't forget The Balladeer. Truth is, Ol' Waylon was there first, and he gets the final word.

BALLADEER (V.O.)
So you see, that's the way it goes in Hazzard. Where the Dukes will even help out the enemy when the chips are down. An' that's plum typical of the Dukes of Hazzard. Too bad it ain't the same everywhere else, huh?
FADE OUT.
THE END

***

The Dukes had a special and unique chemistry, and that's why the show worked even with weak, repetitive storylines, even if the network didn't support us, even when conditions were difficult behind the scenes. The cast members didn't always agree, and we didn't always get along. We did not hang out together much off set.

But on set, we were a team, and we always had each other's back. That's what family is. You may not always get along, and sometimes the storyline doesn't make sense. Some days you don't even like each other. But at the end of the day, you're still a family.

Critics sometimes dismiss *Dukes of Hazzard* as lowbrow entertainment, nothing but short shorts and car jumps. Don't get me wrong; I think there are a lot of worse things in this world than long tan legs and muscle cars flying through the air. But the heart of Hazzard is love amongst family and friends.

"Good Ol' Boy" is not about gender, race, religion, or the place where you were born. It's about being a decent citizen, a good brother or sister or friend. It's about not only helping your neighbor, but also a stranger too, even if it costs you something.

It's about even lending a helping hand to your enemy when the chips are down, because everybody's human, and none of us are above the worst. Help works both ways. Sometimes we give it, and other times, we're the ones in need. And we need to receive help, with dignity.

It's about respect and listening to the wisdom of your elders, saying, "Yes, ma'am" and "No, sir," fighting for what's right, for the less fortunate, for things worth believing in. For letting your word be your bond and never forgetting the things that truly matter in this one short life we live.

Dukes of Hazzard viewers around the world could feel that sense of community. Four decades later, I believe you still can. In some ways now, more than ever.

Final Season Squirrels:

- I was in shopping for shirts in Macy's one day and saw a head towering above the racks. Turns out that seven-foot-two-inch Kevin Peter Hall did not play center for the Lakers, he was a stand-up comedian. I told him that he'd be perfect for an episode of the show I was directing. Kevin loved *Dukes* so he auditioned and became the last villain to ever kidnap Boss Hogg. (Kevin went on to play "Harry" in Harry and the Hendersons and the title role in Predator.)

- Kane Hodder played a ninja in "The Dukes in Hollywood." Kane is known for his role as Jason in Friday the 13th, and *Dukes* was his first job back after getting badly burned during a stunt. Kane and I worked together on Smothered and share the same birthday.

- Bo, Luke, and Daisy – all orphans. After Jimmie Best's birth mother died of tuberculous, he was sent to an orphanage. The woman who leaves her infant son for the Dukes to raise ("A Baby for the Dukes") was played by Jimmie's daughter, Janeen. How many times did we donate our reward to the Hazzard County Orphanage? The orphan theme runs through famous works such as David Copperfield, Oliver Twist, Quasimodo, Queen Elsa, James Bond, Harry Potter, Frodo Baggins, Batman, Clark Kent, Clubber Lang, Snow White, Tom Sawyer, Tarzan, Little Orphan Annie, Luke, Leia, Han Solo, and Rey. The orphan is an underdog, forced to find his or her place in the world, making his or her way, the only way they know how. Something to think about.

- That "final scene" at the Boar's Nest wasn't our last. We only staged it that way for the Entertainment Tonight cameras and still had a couple of days left to shoot. The last scene ever shot for *The Dukes of Hazzard* was on process day with me and Tom in the General Lee. Unlike the televised ending where we all hugged at the Boar's Nest, I remember saying, "Well, that's a wrap." The rear projection screen went blank, and I cried like a baby behind the wheel of that engine-less General.

REUNION! CARRYING ON (LIKE WE DID BEFORE)

"Shows tend to end when they're over. The Dukes of Hazzard
has not ended for the fans, and it has not ended for the cast
or the crew. I'm very proud to be a part of that."
— John R. Schneider

Discussions for a return to *Dukes of Hazzard* began a few years after the show ended. Gy Waldron developed his first reunion script in 1988 and pitched it to CBS, but they passed. The thought had been bouncing around in my head as well, and I wrote up a treatment for a reunion, hoping that Warner would develop *Dukes* into a full-length film. I wanted to have the Duke boys return as NASCAR's top driver and crew chief and finally tell the story of how Bo, Daisy, and Luke came to live with Uncle Jesse after the train accident that claimed the lives of their parents. There was a lot of talk about bringing back *The Dukes*, but as far as Warner Bros. and CBS were concerned, it was only talk.

I was pursuing opportunities in filmmaking at the time and even tried to buy the rights so we could do it ourselves. To me, a *Dukes of Hazzard* reunion seemed like the biggest no-brainer in Hollywood.

But Hollywood did not agree.

In February 1994, Sorrell Booke passed away at his home in Sherman Oaks and was buried at Hillside Park, the beautiful old Jewish cemetery in Culver City. The inscription on his stone reads: BELOVED PA, GRANDPA, BROTHER AND BOSS.

Sorrell played many roles in his career but none so dear as Jefferson Davis Hogg. I set out to show a bit more of Sorrell in Boss Hogg for our final *Dukes* episode, but truth is, it was there all along. Fans couldn't help but love him. They knew that deep down, as corrupt and greedy as Boss could be, there was good in there to boot. When you can love the villain too? That's storytelling at its best, a testimony to the talent of Sorrell Booke.

There's an old saying in the South that weddings bring out the worst in people while funerals bring out the best. Time slips away from us all, but a funeral is the one place where we slow down and remember what matters, at least for a little while.

The cast gathered that afternoon to pay our last respects, and as I stood there with Jimmie, Denver, Cathy, Sonny, Rick, Tom, and Ben, one thing seemed sure: the chemistry between us remained. We were still a family, and we missed each other and missed the show. The time for a reunion was now, before we lost anyone else. If only we could get the studio on board...

Fast-forward to '96. In an attempt to entice a younger crowd, The Nashville Network forked over ten million dollars for syndication rights to the original series. *The Dukes of Hazzard* quickly became TNN's highest-rated show, beating every other cable network in its time slot. Not only that, *Dukes* reruns drew the lucrative eighteen to thirty-four demographic, pulling in even more young viewers than MTV. (Reports circulated of a *Dukes* drinking game on college campuses. Every time there's a car jump, Dixie horn or shot of Daisy's legs, take a drink.)

Some said that *Dukes* was back, but I knew we'd never really left in the first place. *Dukes of Hazzard* was an essential part of Americana. Kids born after the show were still pretending to be Duke boys, jumping their dirt bikes and shouting, "YEE-HAA!", fighting the system like modern-day Robin Hoods. Adults were building their own custom versions of the General Lee. Each Halloween brought a new crop of Bo, Daisy, Luke, and Boss Hogg costumes. And summertime was always accompanied by a bumper crop of Daisy Dukes.

If anything, the show's legacy had grown deeper with time. And after meeting thousands of *Dukes* fans, I can say this: *Dukes* fans are of *all* backgrounds and beliefs. Girls, boys, black, white, straight, gay, rich, and poor, from all around the world. The PC police can try to put their pretentious and judgmental spin on the show (because they so desperately need to feel superior) – but *Dukes* was universal. And I say, still is.

***

The show continued to be a winner for TNN, and people were buzzing about *The Dukes* once again. New action figures hit stores along with a ton of updated merchandise. *Hazzard* was hot, and Warner Bros. was suddenly on board with bringing the cast back for one more run.

They gave us the green light on a script by Gy Waldron, turned Warner Studio's Midwest Street back into Hazzard Square, and in December 1996, the original cast and crew of *Dukes of Hazzard* came together again. More than twelve years had passed since we shot our final episode, but from the first day of filming, it felt like slipping into your favorite pair of old jeans.

Not that there weren't some old, familiar problems as well. *Dukes* still seemed to be the studio's snot-nosed orphan. The budget they gave us was so tight that we had to make do with three Dodge Chargers leftover from the original show. Paul Baxley returned to coordinate stunts, but since we had only three Generals, he couldn't do any car jumps. Instead, we recycled footage from the old series, including Jack Gill's barnbuster jump and Gary Baxley's record-breaker at the Santa Clarita River.

The studio wouldn't recreate the Duke family farmhouse, so we had to use a two-story structure from the Warner lot that was actually the back porch of what used to be Boss Hogg's home. The original Boar's Nest "burned," and the Hazzard sheriff's station was a hand-me-down too. Waylon was offended by the amount they offered him to return, so country crooner Don Williams stepped in as The Balladeer. Nashville's nicest guy, Steve Wariner, scored our music and produced a new theme song for the reunion, a Wopat/Schneider duet called, "Carryin' On (Like We Did Before)."

In terms of story, we tried not to mess with the *Hazzard* formula. When a nefarious but hair-brained scheme threatens Uncle Jesse's farm, the Duke family reunites. Bar fights, kidnappings, and car chases ensue. In the end, it all comes down to a race, featuring the General Lee.

I dug Bo's yellow cowboy shirt out of my closet; Tom put on his blue plaid snap-down, and Denver slipped back into his original faded overalls, even if his beard was pasted on with latex, and he had to wear a wig under his cap. He'd lost weight due to his fight with lung cancer, so wardrobe put him in the same kind of padding that Sorrell had worn to play Boss Hogg.

Denver was taking chemo during filming and sometimes struggled to remember his dialogue. We all loved on Denver and assured him we would help, but I could tell he was in bad shape. "Don't worry about it," I told him. "We'll make it work. You're Uncle Jesse. We're just glad you're here."

"John, this is important," Denver said, hand on my shoulder, tired, but still with a hint of that twinkle in his eye. "I wouldn't miss it for the world."

He pushed through and showed up every day, eager to bring Uncle Jesse to the fans one last time.

***

Tom and I were back in the General before the rear projection screen with a "tweenie" light overhead for the sun. Wopat told the special effects guy about how we used to rock the car with a two-by-four on an apple cart and throw Fuller's dirt in the fan to simulate driving down a country road. There were some murmurs about how we needed to wrap the scene before lunch, and I heard someone comment from the side, "Why are we going to all this trouble? It's just a TV movie."

"Hold on a minute," I began, bringing production to a halt. "If you think this is just some television movie, then you should leave. This is *The Dukes of Hazzard,* and we're here because people truly *love* this show. We are a part of something that will last for the rest of our lives. For a lot of fans, this is much more than just a show."

The crew member apologized, and I don't think he truly meant any harm. Sometimes you need a little conflict to let people know where things stand.

Dukes of Hazzard: Reunion! debuted at eight Central on April 25, 1997. CBS Friday Night with *The Dukes* was back. Critics turned up their noses at our return, calling the show "cornpone" and its success "puzzling" – but the public sure didn't see it that way. Over fifteen million viewers tuned in to see Bo and Luke fight the system again.

***

After the success of the reunion movie, it was obvious we'd have to do it again. Many fans have asked why they took the Dukes out of Hazzard for the second reunion. Like most things in Hollywood, it's complicated. But the short answer is, money. Regardless of the question, money always seems to be the answer. Sad.

The studio didn't want to pay to shoot out in the country, so the second get-together sent the Duke cousins off to Hollywood to raise funds for

Hazzard Hospital back home. It's pretty inexpensive to film a Hollywood movie inside a film studio. We'd done an episode in season seven called "The Dukes in Hollywood" that was likely an inspiration as well.

Mac Davis played The Balladeer for this outing, and I'll be the first to admit, the script was a little thin. They tried to make it like we were dumb hicks come to the big city, backwoods and clueless enough to camp out beneath the Hollywood sign. We were *The Dukes of Hazzard*, not *The Beverly Hillbillies*. Tom and I tried to suggest changes that would keep it true to the original tone, but it was a battle to do the best we could with what we had to work with.

The second reunion has its moments. We at least spent the first five minutes back in Hazzard Square for a hoedown with Toby Keith, and regardless of the script, the Dukes family was together on TV again. I was still packing my punches for the fight scenes and struggling to keep up with Tom as we slid over the hood and into the windows of the General Lee. Paul Baxley returned to do stunts, and his grandson, Craig Jr., took the General for his final televised flight.

In some ways, it felt like we were coming full circle. Twenty-one years later, the Dukes were back in Griffith Park, the same place we'd taken those first cast pictures back in '78.

***

Fans often ask my feelings about the 2005 feature film and *The Beginning* TV movie for ABC Family in 2007. Honestly, they would have to be better to suck. Burt Reynolds played Boss Hogg in the first remake, and we spoke not long after it came out.

"I'm sorry, John," Burt said. "The movie is crap. I signed on because I loved and understood *Dukes* and hoped we could honor the original show. Apparently, I was the only one who gave a turkey."

That's the moment I became friends with a man I consider one of film history's biggest stars. The man I skipped school, climbed a fence, and lied through my teeth to catch a glimpse of back in '76. I miss Burt every day. He had no patience for all this politically correct nonsense.

The remake projects missed the heart, missed the message. Missed the chemistry by a country mile. Sexy is fine, but trashy in Hazzard County is an insult to the legacy of the show. Apparently, the fans agree, and neither effort is considered a true part of *The Dukes of Hazzard* catalog. The makers even took Jessica, Sean, and Johnny off the following run of die-cast General Lee models and returned to using Tom, Cathy, and John. Take that, Hollywood!

Tom and I played brothers in *Christmas Comes to Willow Creek,* and he made an appearance on *Smallville* as a "good ol' boy," but the closest we've come to a Duke boys reunion is the 2014 commercial for the online marketplace Autotrader.

The commercial was shot single camera in South Louisiana with director Janusz Kamiński. (Two-time Oscar-winning cinematographer for *Schindler's List* and *Saving Private Ryan.*) Kamiński tilted the camera so the flag wouldn't show so as not to ruffle feathers, since it was an ad. In the backstory, it was Cooter who put the battle flag on General Lee. The emblem was part of the Georgia state flag then, and in the first shows, the General had three, one on the roof, another on the front license place, and a third stars and bars crossed with a checkered flag above the decklid. If it was motivated by prejudice, Uncle Jesse would have said, "Git that dang flag offa that car! I don't care if you gotta scratch it off with your fingernails..." Anyone who believes *Dukes* is racist has obviously never watched the show.

The Autotrader spot was a big sensation on television and the internet. There's something magical about me and Tom together in that car. I can't explain it. I never speak with a Southern accent, but the second I see Wopat, we instantly turn into Bo and Luke. Four decades later, I'm still transported to Hazzard County.

I think the success of the Autotrader ad helped fans get over the bad taste from the studio's reboot projects. Rumors began circulating that a new *Dukes* reunion was in the wings, but it wasn't to be. I don't know if it's possible for Warner Bros. to capture the magic again. So, I'll do projects like Bo's Extravaganza and *Christmas Cars* and maybe even another *Collier and Co.* some day. We've got fourth-generation *Dukes* fans now. Hopefully, the legacy will continue to roll on long after we are all gone. My adventures in an orange Dodge Charger aren't over yet.

Denver passed away on Christmas Day, 1997, less than a year after we wrapped shooting on the first reunion film. We dedicated *Hazzard in*

Hollywood to his memory. Waylon died in 2002. Jimmie Best finished the race in 2015 at age eighty-eight. Hardly a day passes that I'm not asked if the remaining *Hazzard* cast will ever get together on screen again.

Even now, the chemistry between us remains.

Reunion Squirrels:

- Gy Waldron was involved in every *Dukes*-related project, from the Moonrunners film in 1975 to 2000's *Hazzard in Hollywood*.

- Look closely and you'll spot a retired General Lee in the 1992 Mel Gibson film Forever Young. The '69 383 Charger is still orange, but the markings were removed, of course. Warner crew turned it back into the General once *The Dukes* reunion was on, and I helped get the details right. For *Hazzard in Hollywood*, we mostly used my Bo's General Lee as the picture car.

- The NAACP threatened to boycott CBS if they didn't remove the rebel flag for the 1997 reunion. CBS respectfully declined; the General kept his flag, and *Dukes of Hazzard: Reunion!* became one of the highest-rated shows of the year, around the world, from Venezuela's *Los Duques del Peligro: La Reunion!* to *Cursa Din Hazzard II* for fans in Romania. Squirrel in a squirrel, our original title was *Return to Hazzard*.

- No, seriously. My yellow shirt in the reunion is the same one I wore in the original series. I still have it. In fact, I'm wearing it on the cover of this book. Guess what? Thanks to brother Bob calling me fat, my "Bo Duke" shirt and jeans still fit. Take that!

ACT III: MUSIC

"I love songs about horses, railroads, land, Judgment Day, family, hard times, whiskey, courtship, marriage, adultery, separation, murder, war, prison, rambling, damnation, home, salvation, death, pride, humor, piety, rebellion, patriotism, larceny, determination, tragedy, rowdiness, heartbreak and love. And Mother. And God."
— Johnny Cash

*"I'd rather fall flat than not try.
I can always get up again."*
— John R. Schneider

NOW OR NEVER

There's always one more way to do things, and that's your way."
— Waylon Jennings

My recording career officially began at age fifteen when the director of Academy Theatre introduced me to Babs Richardson, who owned Atlanta's Mastersound Studios and had worked with artists like Isaac Hayes, Mac Davis, and Pink Floyd. Babs was putting together a soundtrack for the Christmas story, *The Small One,* and needed a young person who could do a booming voice for a song called "The Auctioneer." Academy had just finished production of *The Wizard of Oz,* and since I'd done the voiceover for the Wizard, they thought I might be able to pull it off.

I drove down to their studio on Spring Street, cut a few takes of "The Auctioneer," and recorded dialogue for the story part of the record as Jesus's stepdad, Joseph. Mastersound paid me a hundred dollars for a couple of hours' work, which seemed phenomenal at the time. My first recording session was easy, fun, and it was cool to think I might be singing into the same microphone as Isaac Hayes.

The following year, I toured with Academy Children's Theatre. We did Shakespeare but musicals for kids too, traveling around to schools. I helped build sets and write the score for *Under Odin's Eye,* and also played the part of a Viking. My principal at North Springs gave me school credit for the production, which enabled me to graduate early and pursue show business full-time. Music was always a part of my dream, from the very start, whether I was performing with the Georgia All-State Choir or singing "Stayin' Alive" in white spandex right down the hall from my audition for *Dukes of Hazzard.*

Shooting *Dukes* consumed a lot of time and energy, but I still carried my guitar around and pursued opportunities in music every chance I could. After the show took off, CBS asked me to perform at the 1980 People's Choice Awards. *Rocky II* won Favorite Movie, Burt Reynolds was voted

Favorite Actor, and I sang "Still" by Lionel Richie and the Commodores, which was nominated for Favorite New Song. I think a lot of people were surprised to see that I could do something other than fistfight bumpkins and shout YEE-HAA while jumping a Dodge Charger over a creek. They didn't know that I'd spent years paying dues in music, too.

There was some industry buzz around my performance of "Still," and Scotti Brothers Records brought me into the studio to see if I could really sing. It was like Warner flying me out to screen test for *Dukes*. You can be good performer live and still suck in the studio.

Scotti Brothers had me cut the disco hit, "Love Is in the Air." Some singers choke under the pressure of vocal booths, fancy microphones, and producers staring at you through the glass while you try to hit the right notes. Didn't bother me one bit. The studio felt like home to me, a place where I had always belonged. Like it was all part of the plan.

Apparently, the record label liked what they heard enough to sign me to a multi-album deal. I'm not sure what happened to my version of "Love Is in the Air." Hopefully, it still exists in a studio vault somewhere.

Scotti Brothers had a big hit with Leif Garrett, so they tried to steer me toward the kind of teen pop that had been successful for other young actor/singers like John Travolta and David Cassidy. The label would send over eleven songs and say, "Pick ten and tell us which day you can come in to record them." It wasn't exactly the album I wanted to make, but it was an opportunity, and I was excited to work with producer Robie Porter, who'd made some great hit records for Air Supply.

I would do twelve-hour days on *The Dukes* set, then drive down Santa Monica to Pico Boulevard and spend another six at the recording studio. Turns out Robie was a big fan of Hank and Elvis and had been in the Western classic *Daniel Boone*, so we got along fine.

The *Now or Never* album was released the following spring, and the first single, a cover of Elvis's "It's Now or Never," went top five on radio while the album cracked *Billboard*'s Top Ten. With my debut's success, Scotti Brothers rushed me back into the studio to record *White Christmas*. Like television, Christmas projects are usually done in the summer so producers can have them ready in time for the holiday season. In fact, as I'm writing this, it's ninety-six degrees, and I was just in my back yard with a jacket on to film a scene for *Christmas Cars*. (Look for the sweat and listen for our Balladeer, Johnny Lee, saying, "It was the hottest Christmas since the War of Northern Aggression." Take that, revisionist historians!)

The only two things I remember about the *White Christmas* album is that I took the ugly sweater cover photos in New York while filming *Dream House*, and I wanted to acknowledge my roots by recording a barbershop quartet version of "O Little Town of Bethlehem." Either Scotti Brothers couldn't find a quartet, or they didn't want to pay one, so the arranger wrote out all four parts, and I sang them myself. I was my own one-man quartet.

***

Life was a whirlwind then, filming *Dukes* and movies, touring to promote records, making special appearances in whatever spare time I had left. I was guest-host on *The Midnight Special* featuring Donna Summer and Dottie West, sang an *Oklahoma* medley with *Mork & Mindy's* Pam Dawber for NBC's *All-Star Salute to the American Musical*, and even worked with George Burns on a revisit of the *Texaco Star Theatre*.

My third album, *Quiet Man*, was released in April '82. One of my original compositions, "I Need Someone to Miss," made the record, and the title track was written especially for me as a tribute to John Wayne.

John's son, Michael, took me to lunch at the Smoke House in Burbank to tell me how much he appreciated the song. In turn, I told Michael how much his dad's work meant to me. I don't even know if I would be in show business if not for John Wayne. I might be "Bo Duke," but he was *The* Duke, and one major regret is that I never got to meet my hero. John Wayne wasn't afraid to speak his mind, and he wasn't offended if somebody else spoke theirs. I wonder what he would think of the world today.

Hee Haw invited me on the show that October. There's no telling how many times Tom Wopat and I sat in the General Lee between takes, blowing raspberries while singing "Pfft, You Were Gone." It was a boyhood dream of mine to stand in that famous kornfield and swap jokes with the Hee Haw Honeys. I must have done okay, because a couple of months later, they had me back again. And again, and again...

Around that time, I met a Laurel Canyon songwriter named Michael

Stanton who convinced me I could sing straight country. Up to that point, I'd focused mostly on Broadway and pop. I loved Stanton's work enough to record an entire project of his songs and pay for it out of my own pocket. Scotti Brothers loved it too and chose the sessions to be my fourth LP.

If You Believe came out in the summer of '83, and we took the cover photos on the porch of the Beaudry clan's cabin from season five's "Daisy's Shotgun Wedding." (Note the deer antlers.) I borrowed a shirt from wardrobe and walked through the Valencia/Hazzard dust in my Bo Duke jeans and boots. If you look closely, you can see a mic antenna still taped to the heel of my boot.

The record label put out another Elvis cover for the single, a duet version of "Are You Lonesome Tonight" with an artist from the Scotti Brothers stable named Jill Michaels. The musical direction was overall better, but the song didn't get much attention from radio. I felt like it was time for a change but still owed Scotti Brothers a few more albums.

Jimmy Bowen heard *If You Believe* about the time he was leaving Elektra Records to take over MCA. Bowen was a legendary figure, having produced Sinatra, Dean Martin, Kenny Rogers, Glen Campbell, Haggard, and Hank Jr. After listening to my record, he offered to buy my contract from Scotti Brothers so he could sign me to MCA. I didn't have to think long and hard about that one. Finally, I was on my way to Music City.

Musical Squirrels:
- Tom and I both had songs on the radio in 1983. "Full Moon, Empty Pockets" was his first for Columbia Records, while "Dreamin'" was my lead-off single from *Quiet Man*.

- The green plaid shirt I'm wearing on *If You Believe* is my Christmas Eve shirt from "The Great Santa Claus Chase."

- My second CBS special aired in December '83. *John Schneider's Christmas Holiday* starred Debbie Allen, The Gatlin Brothers, and Bruce Jenner. We shot in Sun Valley, Idaho, with director Marty Pasetta, who had worked on the Academy Awards and *Elvis: Aloha from Hawaii*.

- Less than four years after "The Auctioneer," I returned to Mastersound's recording studio for *Dukes of Hazzard*. It's where we shot "Daisy's Song." Crazy, huh?

THE LONG WAY HOME

"I discovered what was at the top of the mountain.
Nothing. Not one thing. What was at the top
was all the experiences that you had to get there."
— Lionel Richie

I headed south to make my honky-tonk debut for MCA, but the song pitchers in Nashville offered me nothing but soft pop. "Look, I want a country song," I finally told them. "My dad played in a square dance band called The Crop Dusters. I love Conway Twitty and Johnny Cash."

They dusted off an old demo that had been bouncing around the back alleys of Music Row for years called "I've Been Around Enough to Know." I sat back, listened, and knew I'd found not only the right song, but the right direction for my new record.

Too Good to Stop Now came out in July '84, and Jimmy Bowen had the idea to release "I've Been Around Enough to Know" to America's most influential disc jockeys without my name listed on the label. He wanted them to play it based on their belief in the song and not treat it like a novelty from "Bo Duke." Most DJs guessed the mystery singer was rising star George Strait, but they all agreed to play the single, and sixteen weeks later, I had my first *Billboard* number-one song.

Bowen's plan was a smart move, but I wonder sometimes if debuting as an "unknown artist" is the reason so many fans are surprised to discover I was a successful country singer. Sure, I'll do "Good Ol' Boys" in concert, but I also perform several of my radio hits. It never fails, someone will come up and say, "Wait a minute, that was *you*?! I didn't know you sang…"

"Country Girls" was released as the next single — this time with my name on it — and reached the top of the *Billboard* charts as well. Two number-one songs and a hit album in my first year with MCA. My music career shifted into high gear just as we were wrapping up the final season of *Dukes*.

Good thing too, because I would need it. At age twenty-four, I owed 1.5 million dollars in back taxes.

***

I was in that place where actors who once starred on hit TV shows realize that the money tree is going dry. Or in my case, dried up, died, and fallen across the road. I'd been trying to catch up financially ever since the merchandise/strike fiasco of '83, but it was one of those situations where you're paddling hard and fast but the current still sweeps you downstream.

There was no eighth year of *Dukes* to pay taxes on my income from season seven, so I had to take every possible tour date and sell my Dino Ferrari, the Bora, and my Aston Martin Volante convertible to the Executive Toy Store, an upscale car dealer in Beverly Hills. I don't expect anyone to feel sorry for a guy who had to sell his Maserati to pay taxes, but this is a memoir, and it's all part of the story. I didn't care that much about expensive clothes or houses, but it broke my heart to sell those beautiful cars. I don't even want to think about what they'd be worth now.

How did I get myself in so much trouble? Well, it goes something like this: Entertainers are independent contractors. That means they don't hold taxes out of your check. If you get paid a hundred thousand dollars for doing a movie, you did not make a hundred grand. Accountants, managers, lawyers, agents. They all want their cut first.

Uncle Sam still gets half of your income, so you hustle and pray the phone keeps ringing because you'll need this year's check to pay last year's taxes. I've always been an all-in, live-for-the-day kind of person. The trait that made me jump a fence to get on *Smokey and the Bandit*, the quality that made me perfect for the part of Bo Duke – well, that same quality might also make you not so good at saving for a rainy day. The kid who does his own stunt driving may not be too sharp with tax shelters, deductions, or stashing money aside for the IRS. When you're good at making money but not managing it, you hire people and trust them to help.

If the network doesn't renew your hit show? And your accountant turns out to be crooked? You might be up the creek.

Sure wish I'd have listened to Denver's advice. Money is a powerful force. You can work yourself to death and still end up in debt. So, thank

God for country music.

***

"Country Girls" was still riding high on the charts when MCA released *Tryin' To Outrun the Wind*. (Which in hindsight, was quite the insightful title.) "It's A Short Walk From Heaven To Hell" made the top ten, and I filmed a video for the next single, "I'm Gonna Leave You Tomorrow," at the Crazy Horse in Pomona, California. Nobody was really doing country music videos back then because we didn't have the equivalent of MTV. I paid for it myself and brought the clip to MCA to help promote the single, but they just thought it was cute.

"John, believe us on this one," the label assured me. "Videos will never have anything to do with the sales of country music."

Seemed a little short-sighted to me but well, okay.

Music was a different horse from making television shows. During the tail end of *Dukes*, I might do one or two concerts a week, but now I had a tour bus and usually spent from Wednesday morning until late Sunday night on the road. Singing in smoky barrooms, eating Waffle House at three a.m., trying to catch a few hours' sleep on a Silver Eagle as it rolls through the Rockies at night. Days off tour were spent in the studio, as MCA's strategy was to keep the music coming nonstop. The second single from *Tryin' To Outrun the Wind* wasn't even out of the top ten when my third album, *A Memory Like You*, came out.

1986 was insane. Tawny and I split, *A Memory Like You* became my first number-one LP, and the singles, "What's A Memory Like You (Doing in A Love Like This)" and "You're the Last Thing I Needed Tonight" topped the charts as well. Buck Owens had left *Hee Haw*, so they asked me to co-host a few shows, and I got to do "Pickin' and Grinnin'" with Roy Clark. I shot a remake of John Wayne's *Stagecoach* with Kris Kristofferson, Johnny Cash, Willie, Waylon, and David Allan Coe and returned for Farm Aid II, playing somewhere between Bon Jovi, George Jones, and Rick James. (no joke.)

"You're the Last Thing I Needed Tonight" was still number one in August of '86 as MCA rushed out *Take the Long Way Home*. Cash and Waylon joined me for "Better Class of Losers," and the first single, "At the Sound of the Tone," raced up the charts to number five while the title track went top ten next. I won the "Star of Tomorrow" award at the 20th Annual Music City News Country Awards that year, but as the people clapped and flashbulbs blinded my eyes, it all seemed like one big blur, much like those last few seasons of *Dukes*.

In 1987, *You Ain't Seen the Last of Me* hit stores, and I landed the much-coveted gig of opening for Alabama. Randy and the boys weren't just the biggest band in country music – they were one of the biggest bands on the planet back then. Suddenly, I was playing sold-out stadiums, and at MCA's suggestion, we changed up my show. Country singers in the '80s were starting to look more like rockers, so I let my hair grow long and started wearing bandanas and ripped jeans.

Late one night, we were traveling from a concert in South Florida to a Carolina festival when my tour bus broke down. A devoted fan named Donna happened to be following the bus, so I grabbed my guitar, some merch, loaded my Irish Setter, Diesel, into her car, and we headed for the show in Greensboro. I performed for forty thousand people that night with nothing on stage but my guitar and my dog, who apparently unimpressed, fell asleep by my feet. It turned out to the be one of the best shows on that tour. Still, I couldn't shake the feeling that things were coming to an end.

Even though I was still having hits, the record label's attention had moved to newer acts, and in the era before Soundscan it was impossible to know where you stood. Pop, rock, and R&B had barcodes, but country and Christian music were lagging behind. No barcodes, no way to track sales. I had a number-one album that didn't go gold, while my buddy Dwight Yoakam hit certified platinum without even breaking the top ten. (Gold = 500,000 in sales, platinum means one million.) We were expected to trust whatever the label told us – and I was already burnt from trusting others with my money. The music business was starting to feel like *déjà vu*.

Meanwhile, CBS was trying to lure me back into television with a leading role in a new comedy-action series, *Grand Slam*, about two competing bounty hunters who team up. Sounded good to me.

MCA put out a *Greatest Hits* album, and I told my agent to book me solid until the last Alabama show. After that, I planned to walk away from music for a while. It's always better to leave on your own terms and closer to the top, I believe. I'd done nine albums in less than seven years. It was time to move on to something new.

***

In 2014, I bought an old church campground in south Louisiana to transform into a film studio. Alicia and I worked ourselves ragged rebuilding that swampland into our dream, then a few months later, the floods came and washed it all away. We pulled ourselves together, emptied our pockets, borrowed all we could, and built our dream back from the ground up.

Four months later, everything flooded again. This time, even worse than before.

Kitchen tables underwater, keepsakes and family pictures floating downstream. Video cameras and editing suites caked in mud. One flood? You pick yourself up and drive on. Two floods in a year when things were already falling apart?

I was sitting in the ruins of our living room, mold growing up the walls, still reeling from the extent of the damage. One thing the floodwaters didn't get was my old Martin guitar. I got it back in tune and started strumming the opening riff from "I've Been Around Enough to Know." Alicia walked in so I laid the Martin to the side.

"Why'd you do that?" she asked.

"Playing guitar always used to make me feel better," I replied. "Even when I was a kid, when things were bad, I would play my guitar."

"I wasn't asking why you picked it up," Alicia said. "I was asking why did you put it down?"

I didn't have an answer for that. Not a good one. I thought about Alicia's question a lot over the next few days. In times of struggle or loneliness, when I wasn't sure how to move on, I always turned to my guitar. Now, I'd been out of music for almost thirty years. Maybe I was frustrated with the industry, but music and the music business are two different things. I hate show business, but I love the show. And I have always loved the music.

Leaving music left a hole inside of me, and once I started back, I was eager to make up for lost time. Alicia and I are a force to reckon with, the TTB (Team to Beat.) We had an idea, but it was pretty crazy. But so is climbing Mt. Everest, right? It's cold; it's high. You might die. I'm sure they thought the first person to climb Everest had lost his mind. A key part of pursuing dreams is to ignore the critics. You can have fun and do some amazing things, long as you don't care what anyone thinks. Be fearless. Reckless courage is the key.

In 2018, with the help of producer/drummer Paul Leim, we began a project called *The Odyssey*, in which I planned to release one new song a week for a year. Fifty-two weeks, fifty-two new songs. Just like finding "I've Been Around Enough to Know," I went up and down the back alleys of Music Row looking for the great unheard songs by Nashville's top writers. Not the best "hits" or what might target the right demographic to sell blue jeans or beer. The best *songs*. I even started writing some of my own.

Alicia and I got a place down on Music Row – not where all the high-rise condos and hipster gastropubs sit stacked on top of each other, but over in the old section, at Spence Manor, where Elvis once held court with his Memphis Mafia, and songwriters still craft ballads around the guitar-shaped swimming pool. (No, Elvis never went skinny-dipping in that pool. It's an urban legend. Have I ever enjoyed a moonlight swim after a night of good food and wine at The Standard with my smiling jolie blonde? Well, maybe. But that's a story for another day.)

With a new mission and catalog of great new songs, I set out on the *I Didn't Know You Sang* Tour. We blew past our goal of fifty-two singles in fifty-two weeks and kept going with a Christmas project, an acoustic compilation of hits, my first gospel record, and a collection of hard country. Who knows what the future holds? Maybe I'll even record some barbershop quartet.

Whatever it is, Alicia and I will put it out ourselves. I still refuse to play the game. If you play with us, you play our game. Like Sandy Koufax. He didn't play your game; you played his or got hurt. (I wrote a screenplay called *Facing Koufax* that we'll do one day. It's not about baseball.)

Anyway, back to the story. The music business has radically changed. Now, the artist has the power to go directly to the people. These days, I can wake up, write a song, record it, and release it world-wide before lunch.

Everything works together, I believe. From singing "If I Were a Rich Man" for *Fiddler on the Roof* when I was fourteen to "Redneck Rebel" at fifty-nine. Scotti Brothers opened the door, and Jimmy Bowen taught me how to make a record. It took a flood and Alicia's encouragement for me to pick up my guitar again. I'm still learning, still growing, and still continuing to push. I might outlive my abilities, but I will never outlive my dreams. There's always another mountain to climb.

But if it wasn't for the mountain, who knows where I might be?

Squirrel Odyssey:

- "If It Wasn't for the Mountain" is the single from my first gospel record, 2019's *Recycling Grace*.

- Mickey Gilley had recorded the title track from *Too Good to Stop Now* but liked my version and gave me his blessing. Mickey was still riding high from *Urban Cowboy* in those days. Mickey and Johnny Lee both became good friends of mine. We were excited to get Johnny for *Christmas Cars*.

- If you think *Dukes* used too much rebel flag, check out Alabama in the '80s. Look, it meant something different then. If you try to judge the past by present-day standards, everybody over twenty-five is screwed.

- Cheech Marin was originally supposed to co-star with me in *Grand Slam*, but a movie deal pulled him away. The on-screen chemistry between me and Cheech would have been interesting to see, but I loved working with Paul Rodriguez.

- Just recorded four songs for our next movie, *Stand On It*, a nod to *Smokey and the Bandit*. The Trans Am is gonna be a Hellcat this time. Guess we'll have to cut the T-Tops ourselves.

THE MAN IN BLACK

"We're all in this together if we're in it at all."
— *Johnny Cash*

The first time I ever met Johnny Cash in person was while making the movie *Stagecoach* out in Mescal, Arizona. We were on the set, and it was my first day, and I looked up and saw the man in black. I couldn't wait to tell him what a fan I was and how excited I was to be working in the movie with him. I was on my way to go over there to introduce myself, but he beat me to it and came over to me first, stuck out his hand, and said that famous line of his.

"Hello... I'm Johnny Cash."

I said, "Well, hello... I'm John Schneider, and I know who you are!"

"And, I know who you are," he said.

He wanted to let me know that he and June watched *Dukes of Hazzard* every Friday night and that he was a fan of mine before I could tell him how much a fan of his I was.

Johnny and I became the best of friends right away, right then from the start. I think if you go back and watch *Stagecoach* now you can see that we have an easy chemistry between the two of us. It was never about me hanging out with a personal legend of mine or someone I had looked up to all of my life. It was like two good buddies who just enjoyed spending time together. Like we'd been riding along on the front of the stagecoach all of our lives. It was something to be in a movie with all of these living legends together in one production. Here I was making one of my first movies, and not only was I there with Johnny Cash but it had Willie Nelson, Kris Kristofferson, and Waylon Jennings, too!

Johnny and I were supposed to write a song together for the movie, but the producers ended up using only Willie Nelson's song. At that time, I had a number-one album and was recording another one and was very much in the music scene at that point in my life. It was funny because at the end of the movie after we'd wrapped, Johnny turns to me and asks, "Well, now what are you gonna do?"

I told him I was gonna rent a place in Nashville because I was recording another new album. Then he asked me if I was gonna go on tour with it, and I told him I was. He said, "Well, it's silly for you to pay for a place when your touring so much. You should just come stay with me and June. We've got a big old house out in Hendersonville just outside of Nashville."

I told him he better be careful what he was offering because I'd actually do it, and, of course, being Johnny he said, "Well, I wouldn't ask you if I didn't mean it." That's how he was. So that's what I did.

That's how I ended up moving in and living with Johnny and June Cash. A couple weeks later I showed up. Here I am just a young man, just a few years away from that crazy trick I pulled auditioning to get on *The Dukes of Hazzard*, and now I'm at Johnny Cash's door with my suitcase in my hand, and I'm not here to visit – I'm moving in! I've got my mom on one arm and my Grandma Dugan on the other arm. I think they wanted to see if I had just made up the whole thing about moving in with Johnny Cash because surely something like this just couldn't be true. It was one thing for me to be a star on *Dukes of Hazzard*, to have a number-one album, and to be making movies. But to be moving in with a living legend like Johnny Cash just couldn't be real, but somehow it didn't feel unexpected to me. I was on the right track and somehow I knew it.

Johnny opens the door with a white shirt on because they had just gotten back from Jamaica. He introduced himself to my mom and Grandma Dugan like they needed an introduction, but when I took a step to come in, he said, "Hold up! I need to tell you something." I thought, '*Uh, oh. What have I done wrong? I haven't even been here two minutes.*' Then he turned and said to my mom and grandma, "I hope y'all are hungry 'cause June's got food in the drawer."

That's what he called the food warmer they had, the food drawer. June always had something in the food warmer for people when they came over. Just being hospitable, you know. Then he turned back to me and said, "Before you come in here I want you to know if I ever catch you treating this house like it's not your house, you're no longer welcome in it."

That's the kind of heart he had. John made sure that I felt just that comfortable, like everything he had in the house was mine. I could go in every room and pick up every guitar. I never walked around nervous or worried I was going to break something. And I took him at his word. From that day forward, I walked into that house like I was home because I was.

Grandma Dugan and Mom spent the day sitting around, visiting, and sharing stories with Johnny and June. They didn't move in with me, although I bet they wanted to. But they did spend the whole day, and I remember sitting there just watching all of it as it was happening like it was totally a dream. Here is my mom sitting up in Johnny Cash's house big as you please, and my Grandma Dugan is laughing and telling stories about how she and I used to watch Johnny's show every night from her house. Then she told him about how I'd play my guitar and imitate him singing "A Boy Named Sue." We had a great visit.

I moved in and lived with Johnny and June for about a year and half. If I had moved out in just a few months or something like that, it would have truly been an insult to them. So I ended up living there for a long time. The blue room was my room. I finally moved across the street in a cabin of his.

John had a real easy way of being, just down to earth. If he came walking up in the yard, you'd think he was there to fix the mower or something. You just didn't see this person who was famous all around the world. You just saw a regular guy. Sometimes we'd go fishing, and he'd catch fish after fish, and then he'd suddenly realize we'd been talking and catching fish, and he was supposed to be somewhere.

"Oh, I got to go be in the studio right now recording," he'd say.

We'd hurry up and get off the lake, and he'd throw the fish in the trunk of the Mercedes, and then we'd take off down the road. In the same way that he was so down to earth, he was also great at putting on his coat and getting ready to walk on stage. Just before he walked out there, you could see something come over him. I watched it happen again and again. He became Johnny Cash, the legend. And that's a big part of who he was also.

When we were hanging out, though, it wasn't about the music business or the movies. It wasn't about the work we did. It was about respite. About not having to deal with who you were or who people thought you were supposed to be. It was just two friends hanging out, talking about movies and books, and it was so real. If you imagine being with one of your heroes or somebody you've looked up to or idolized all your life, then that seems impossible that it could be like that, but that's what it was. It was true friendship, and it stayed that way for the rest of our lives. He'd see me and say, "C'mon and go with me to the UK and be in the Wembley Music Festival." And I'd say, "Okay." And, I'd just do it.

Years later, I went back to Nashville to record a record and went to hang out with John just to visit with him, and he asked me, "Do you have any songs on your new album where somebody could sing a duet 'cause I'd love to sing one with you." We'd already recorded "Better Class of Loser's" on my album in 1987, but that had been a while.

"Heck, yeah," I told him, "we'll make one work." So, that's what we did. We recorded a song called "Hell, This Ain't Heaven."

So, for those years I just knew that he was my best friend, and I'm pretty darn sure I was his best friend during that time. You know you have to deal with a lot of things being a public personality sometimes, and it's just stuff that comes with the territory and the blessing. But it was so good for us to be able to sit down behind closed doors and just be home and look at one another in the eye and know where we were coming from. It was nice to be able to relax with someone who totally understood what you were dealing with when you walked out the door.

One story about John I love to share is when we were just hanging out one afternoon in a little room there at his house, and we were looking at some old coins or some Civil War buttons or something because he collected some interesting things. The security guy comes in and delivers this big box to John that had just arrived.

John opens it and says, "Oh good, I had Manuel to make me another duster."

Manuel Cuevas is a designer who made clothes for a lot of famous people like John Wayne, Hank Williams, and George Jones. Manuel dressed Clint Eastwood for his classic Westerns, made the Lone Ranger's mask, and made Elvis's famous gold lame suit. He was the man who put Johnny in black, and John just loved his work.

When Johnny pulled out this duster he said, "Yep, that's exactly what I wanted."

I was quite a bit taller than John, but he was long-waisted, and our arms where the same length. It's a new black duster from Manuel that is just one of the most beautiful things I've ever seen.

"Go ahead; try it on," he said.

So I tried this duster on, and it's fantastic. I'm standing there in this duster that Manuel has made for Johnny Cash. And it was just amazing. It fit perfectly.

Then Johnny tells me, "You keep it."

I protest and tell him, "No, no. You just said it was your favorite. I can't keep this."

He gets this funny smile on his face, and he says, "If it wasn't my favorite, I wouldn't give it to you."

That's what he was like. It's just a perfect story to capture the essence of who Johnny was and what he was about. But it doesn't end there. I kept hearing all these stories about these legends getting these dusters made from Manuel, so I decide to have one made for myself. About seven or eight months after Johnny gave me his duster, I asked Manuel to make a duster out of the legs of some old jeans of mine that my great-grandmother had sown patches on. This is when Manuel was still out in Hollywood before he moved to Nashville. And so he took these old patched-up jeans and made me this gorgeous duster. He made the shoulders out of leather. I mean, it was something nice. I wore it in the photo for my next album cover, *Tryin to Outrun the Wind.*

It's about eight months later *and* Johnny and I are hanging out backstage during Fan Fair week in Nashville, and I've got the duster on.

"Wow," he says. "That's a beautiful duster. Did Manuel make that?"

"Yes," I told him. "And it's is my most favorite piece of clothing I've ever owned." Then I told him about the way Manuel had used those old jeans patched by my great-grandmother. Then I took it off and held it out to him and said, "Here try it on."

Of course, it fit him perfectly, and when he started to take it off, I said, "Oh, no, no. You keep that."

"Oh, no I couldn't do that," he said. "It's your favorite."

And, I told him, "If it wasn't my favorite, I wouldn't give it to you."

Then he got that smile of his because he knew I was just doing for him what he had done for me. The very next album cover he shot, he wore that duster on the cover. That was his way of saying thank you and honoring the gift. I like to think in his way he was honoring my great-grandmother, too.

I didn't meet Johnny in person until that day we were on the set of *Stagecoach*, but I'd been watching his show for years with Grandma Dugan. One of the first impressions I ever did as a kid was of Johnny singing "A Boy Named Sue." I just loved that song, and I'd play it and sing it over and over.

After John passed away, the U.S. Post Office had a stamp created for him in his honor. They had a big celebration service to coincide with the release of it at the Ryman Auditorium in Nashville. I was just standing backstage watching the show when Johnny's son, John Carter, asked me, "What are you gonna sing?" I told him, "I'd love to sing. but nobody asked me," and he said, "Well, I'm asking you."

So, I went out there and sang "A Boy Named Sue." The same song I'd been playing in Grandma Dugan's living room all those years ago imitating Johnny Cash, only now I was singing it at one of the most iconic theaters in the country, the original home of the Grand Ole Opry and doing it as a tribute to him. When I went backstage he said, "Now there's only two people in the world that have ever sung that song on the Ryman stage. You and my dad. And you're the only one that didn't use cue cards." It was just such a pleasure to be able to do that for John.

Years after Johnny and I had been friends for a long time, Waylon Jennings asked me one night, "Do you want to know what it was about you that impressed Johnny so much when he first met you?"

"Well, yeah, I would!'

Then he told me a story that took me all the way back to those days when we were first filming *Stagecoach*. Back all those years ago when I'd first met the legend, Johnny Cash. Where I was standing in the hot desert town of Mescal, Arizona, just starting my career.

We'd been doing some rehearsals on the set before the cameras started rolling. I'm pretty tall, and I saw during rehearsal when we sat down on the stagecoach it was noticeable. The crew had put a pillow down on the stagecoach for each of us. Sitting on that it made me look taller than Johnny, and I just wouldn't have it. *Nobody should be taller than Johnny Cash in a movie.* I tried to be careful so nobody would notice, and when I thought no one was looking, I slipped my pillow out from under me and put it under

Johnny's pillow. That way I wouldn't be sitting on one at all, and he would be sitting up a little higher with two pillows. I didn't think anyone saw me do it, but Waylon had noticed, and so had Johnny. They'd been across the way over on the set and had been watching me, but I just hadn't realized it.

When it was time for the cameras to start filming, Johnny came back over, and we went on making the movie. We spent the next two weeks together on top of that stagecoach, and he was sitting on those two pillows, and he never brought up a thing about it, and neither did I. Waylon kinda laughed about it when he told me the story. I realized then I hadn't gotten away with anything. But, that was all right by me. I didn't think anybody needed to be taller than one of my heroes, Johnny Cash. And, I made certain of it. Someone asked me once if I had three wishes in life what they would be. Spending more time with Johnny would be right up there in the top three. And I wish he and June could have met Alicia. That would have meant a lot to them to see that "special something" we have like they always did.

ACT IV:
INTO THE FUTURE

"We all have our time machines.
Some take us back; they're called memories.
Some take us forward; they're called dreams."
— Jeremy Irons

"Be prepared, but then be ready to jump."
— John R Schneider

SUPERHEROES AND GIVING IT ALL YOU GOT

"A true hero isn't measured by the size of his
strength, but by the size of his heart."
– Zeus

There's never been a time that the world didn't need heroes. And there's never been a better hero than a simple, working man. That's why playing the role of Jonathan Kent on *Smallville* meant a lot to me. Kent embodies a lot of things I believe in and and his values reflect the ways I try to live my life. But I almost passed on the part without ever reading it. It was another one of the roles I was born to play, and I nearly missed it.

"John, we want you to come in and read," Warner Bros. kept saying.

"Superman's already been done," I told them. "The world doesn't need another Superman."

They kept after me about the part so, finally I gave in and said, "All right, I'll look at the script, but I can't imagine it's going to change my mind."

I got halfway through the script and thought it was the best thing I had read.

I called and said, "If this is what the show is going to be, I'll do whatever it takes to be in this project."

At that point, I was one of Warner Bros. three choices for the role, but I knew I had to become their only choice. It wasn't just that the writers could say, *Yes, we want John*. I had to win over everyone on the project. This meant I needed to go through the network audition process. I flew out to L.A. and read for the producers and got the part. I became Jonathan Kent, Superman's father, one of the most iconic roles of my lifetime.

Smallville was so beautifully shot and well-written that it gave Warner Bros. an identity at a key time in television and, I believe it was the beginning for the mega-successful superhero franchises we've seen since. People could see that *Smallville* had heart and soul and history and legend, and it didn't steer too far away from what fans of the source material already knew.

The big question back then was, could it last? Could this new take on Superman have longevity? Warner Bros. put nearly six million dollars into the pilot so, it was incredibly expensive, but it was beautifully done. That's a huge price tag for a TV show, but the pilot was two hours long, the same as a feature-length movie. As an actor, I was happy to know that the studio was all in.

At that point I had teenagers and a tween in the house, so I felt like I had a good handle on what parenting should be and also in some ways what it should not. I told *Smallville* writers Miles Milar and Al Gough how impressed I was with the writing and that I loved the role. "I have kids at home," I said to them. "You know I have my own take on parenting. I'm going to have to bring it to the role." There's a difference between how you parent your first little ones and how you parent a teenager. By the time they are teenagers they are their own people with their own worlds and issues. You don't wait with bated breath until your teen gets home from school, hand him or her a snack, and ask how their day was!

I started talking about how Clark Kent, this orphaned infant with superpowers from another planet is in many ways like a special needs child. I thought his father should be very strict but also very loving. I took this very seriously and gave a lot of energy in communicating with the writers what I thought Johnathan would actually be doing and thinking.

The entire *Smallville* series was shot on location in Vancouver, Canada. It's a beautiful country and I would have loved to have spent more time there, but because I was a dad in real life too, I was commuting from Canada every single week so that I could be there for my kids. I didn't want to play a great father on television and neglect my duties back home.

For five years I made the long trip to Canada to film the show. At the time, I didn't realize that while I was playing the role of Clark Kent's father, I was also being a sort of stand-in dad for a lot of children who were tuning in and had an awful family life, kids who were just trying to hang on to make it through the day.

Years later, I was at Comic-Con, and this young man shook my hand. I could tell by the way that he lingered that he had something he needed to say, so I stopped and gave him all my attention. "I had a really terrible childhood. My father was an awful man, and my family was all screwed up," he confessed. "And if it weren't for Jonathan Kent and *Smallville*, I honestly don't think I would've made it to my teenage years."

When someone offers you a gift like that, all you can do is wrap your arms around them and say, "Thank you."

You work to tell great stories and make beautiful pictures with meaning or maybe just to be entertaining and help someone unplug for a while and relax. Then someone tells you their personal story, gives a testimony to the part you played in changing their lives. It's a humbling process and one that reminds me why we work so hard to get things right.

In the middle of shooting a scene, you're focused on giving your best in that moment, doing everything you can to bring that character to life. Look at the history of Superman. First, it was the comic books, and then the George Reeves television show, and by the time *Smallville* came, an entire Superman universe existed. Jonathan and Martha Kent represented a bedrock of all-American family values – honesty, integrity, and hard work. That was an important trait of the character for me. Jonathan Kent was a hard-working farmer with dirt and calluses on his hands, much like Denver Pyle's Uncle Jesse in *Dukes*.

If you go back and watch *Smallville,* you'll see that when Clark comes home, his dad is always just coming in from the fields or taking his work gloves off to pour himself a cup of coffee. I wanted the character to be real flesh and blood – totally believable. I don't know many hard-working dads who are pacing the floor, waiting for their teenage son to get off the bus so they can have cookies with him. They're trying to figure out how to put bread on the table and keep a roof over their family's head at night. That's the real world, and those are the elements in a character that ordinary people can relate to. Jonathan was patient and caring as a father, but you understood he was a working man. He was trying to take care of everyone and in that way he was not just a minor character on the show.

No one's life is menial or unimportant. Regardless of what role I play, I think about how everyone is significant. It's one of the principles we stick by when making films at John Schneider Studios. Everybody plays an important part in the stories that touch our lives.

Whether you're in a good mood or a bad mood or even tired, it doesn't matter. Acting is giving one-hundred percent to the process because what you commit to film will last forever. Long after I'm gone, people will be watching *Smallville, The Dukes of Hazzard*, and the other work that I've done.

I'm not here to preach, but I believe that principle carries over to the way we live our lives as well. There are no minor parts or lesser characters or unimportant jobs. Everything we do lasts, and it counts, and we never know how one small favor or kindness will forever change someone's life.

One of my favorite *Smallville* experiences was directing *Talisman* in season three. Clark had been stabbed by an ancient knife made of Kryptonite. Martha and Johnathan come home to find Clark bleeding to death on the kitchen floor.

I framed a special shot where Martha slips on something on the floor. She looks down and sees that it's her son's blood. Small details like that give the actor something very real to work with. Storytelling is in the details, those small nuances that make a moment real, and the cast on *Smallville* were open to exploring the art of that scene, to see what made the Kent family tick.

Clark is bleeding to death on the floor, and Jonathan lays hands on him to try to stop the blood. Suddenly, there is a rush of light and power, and Clark is healed. It was the father's love that healed him. Jonathan and Martha sit on the floor with Clark, holding him as he finally wakes up. You feel the love and concern, how tired and worried they've been. They wrap a red blanket around his shoulders. Clark comes around, his strength coming back. He leaps up and runs out, whole again. I designed the shot so that the red blanket is on his shoulders for just a fleeting second when he stands before it falls into his father's lap. Jonathan pauses and takes a long, meaningful look at the red blanket.

Flash forward to the final episode. It's Johnathan who gives Clark his cape. I told the writers that I wanted to be the one to pass Clark's cape to him. That moment felt important to me. The writers and director loved the idea, wrote it into the scene and shot it that way. It was a reminder that no matter where you go, no matter how strong you are, or how famous you may become, you have to remember your roots. Never forget where you came from and the people who supported you and made you who you are today.

To quote the words of a good friend of mine, "You could be the world's greatest hero or its most mild-mannered citizen, but the only person who can write your story is you." Thanks, Miles and Al. That there is an exceptional line of dialogue!

IT'S NOT WHO YOU KNOW; IT'S WHO YOU ARE

"Good acting is good acting, whether it's on stage, on TV, or in film."
— Cody Fern

Because of how many movies and televisions series I've been in, people are always asking me for acting advice. I can tell you one of the most important lessons I've I learned, and that's a lesson I picked up in my early days of doing musical theater. It is a lot of work actually getting the work. You have to stay on top of casting calls and look for jobs all the time. For the last thirty years, my job has been primarily being an employed actor. Just think about that. How many of your favorite television stars kinda went away, and you never heard from them again and wondered where they'd gotten off to? Looking for work is a constant when you think about the nature of this job. There are a lot of ups and down, but one thing you can't do is just sit around, look at the wall, and wait for your agent or some producer to call you. I refuse to not work, and I stay aware of opportunities all the time. I also don't box myself in when it comes to typecasting myself. I don't allow myself to think, *Oh, I can't do that because it's not a lead role,* or *I can't do it because I won't be playing the good guy.* Whatever it is, I'll believe I'll get a job because when it comes down to it, I can't imagine not acting or making movies. It's what I was created to do.

A lot of times people like to think it's who you know, but it's not who you know: it's who you are. There's something about some people where they'll walk in a room, and you'll think *That's the guy!* Maybe it's personality, or it's passion, I'm not sure what *it* is, but *it* sure is something real. You have to believe in yourself with every ounce of courage. You have to pull off surviving in this business, and that shows you who you are down deep inside.

Of course, I was cast on *The Dukes of Hazzard* at a very young age, and yes, I pulled off one of my greatest acting jobs just auditioning for the role of Bo Duke. You know the story. I was that beer-guzzling, boot-wearing, truck-driving guy from Snailville, Georgia. That's what I call acting. I have

145

to say, I made it look so natural it seemed like it was the easiest thing in the world. Like there were no acting skills required at all. I have to hand it to the cast because I think everyone on the show made it look so natural, viewers thought we actually were those characters.

I've always kinda had the notion that if I had grown up in the South, auditioned, and gotten a role as a New York cop in a series, then people would have said, "Wow, that took some great acting skills to pull that off." But here I was from New York, a kid who grew up riding the city bus and playing on sidewalks instead of out in the woods, and I played a fast car-driving hillbilly racing down a dirt road. People might not have considered that acting at the time. When it comes down to it, I think we just made it look like so much fun, it just *couldn't* be acting.

Another thing that can trip you up a little bit in this business is to think that once you've been in a movie or a series that it will be easy from there on out. I think it's actually the opposite of that. I think if you are cast in something that becomes a hit, then people identify you so much as that character, it becomes difficult for them to imagine you as someone else. So that makes it a little bit harder the next time you go out to audition for something, and you're in front of casting directors or producers wanting to make something. It takes something to shake them up to not see you as the character you played when you are someone as well-known around the world as Bo Duke. So, it was a different kind of challenge coming from already being a success. The idea is that you are meant to be a chameleon as an actor. That you can take on any role and bring that character to life.

I've played great guys like the character of Jonathan Kent, but I've also played notoriously bad guys. I was a porn producer on the hit show, *Nip Tuck,* but when I went to audition for that role, no one wanted to see me for that part because I was the good guy. It took a lot of convincing on my team's part for me to even get the audition. They were expecting some smiling hillbilly or this farmer from Kansas, and the character, Ram Peters, was far, far from that. The producers thought they knew exactly who John Schneider was and had told my team, "No, no, not John Schneider. He's too nice. He won't be right for this part." They changed their minds when I walked in the door to meet them, acting like the sleazy character this guy was. In the television series, *Dirty, Sexy Money,* I play another sort of low-life character. When I auditioned, I purposefully made certain that I was just a little too, touchy feely. It's like when you meet someone, and they reach out during an initial meeting and lay a hand on your shoulder then leave it there just a little too long. I did that successfully a number of times, but there was one time that it backfired on me.

I went in character for a show called *Twelve Miles of Bad Road* for a part of a billionaire ass who doesn't need anyone and doesn't care. I went into the meeting acting exactly like that, and then word came back where they said, "Wow, we didn't know John Schneider was such an asshole. He came in here like he didn't care anything at all about this part." See, I was acting, but they thought I really was that guy. It just doesn't feel right to me, though, to walk into a room and shake hands with producers being this great, friendly guy next-door, and then suddenly you try to get into character to officially audition.

The theory is you want them to remember you. There's a lot of competition out there, so you want to stand out, and yes, sometimes you may have to push the envelope and be a little shocking. This is especially true when you are somebody who's played a role that's become an icon. You're trying your best to audition, and they're thinking, "Oh, my God! It's Bo Duke! I had his Underoos." You do whatever you can so that people cannot, and will not, forget you. As old and corny as it may sound, you don't get a second chance to make a first impression.

Chances are, if you are auditioning for a role, it's going to be for either film or the stage. They're two different animals, and you need to know that you are auditioning in two very different kinds of ways. For instance, in a television audition, you have to be very intimate with the camera; your motions are smaller, but the intensity is still there. As a matter of fact, it can be downright smoldering. When you are up there on stage, you have this big space to operate in. You have to play it a little larger. What's funny is when you see someone doing Broadway acting on television because it doesn't work.

Of course, my early days of playing in *Li'l Abner* and being in acting camp at Lake Sunapee gave me a great education for being on stage. And playing the lead more than once in *Fiddler on the Roof* prepared me for feeling comfortable in character, and I went on to join a professional theater company in Atlanta. I was able to be in some of the greatest stage plays of all time like *Fiddler on the Roof, Our Town, The Odd Couple, The Pajama Game,* and of course, *Annie Get Your Gun.*

Even though I had been on stage for so many years already, I actually made my Broadway debut playing the character Baron Felix Von Gaigernin in the musical *Grand Hotel.* I was able to perform that show four hundred and eighty seven times. Performing on stage is very challenging in different ways from performing on a series. Every night the audience is different; they bring something unique to the performance, so it is never the same twice. I was able to perform with the incredible Cyd Charisse, which was a wonderful honor. That many performances is a lot of time spent on that stage and backstage, so naturally you get to know the castmates pretty well. You become a kind of eccentric family. Everyone is doing so many things, and backstage it is so busy with costumers, make-up artists, extras, technical people, and so forth. It's very, very busy back there, but everyone has the same goal, and that is, of course, the show must go on.

Out of all the relationships I made with the cast on *Grand Hotel* during all those rehearsals and performances, the one that became the most profound was that with my dresser, Otis. A dresser is a member of the costume department, and he or she is assigned to particular actors to assist with the wardrobe preparation and changes. He was such a wonderful man, so encouraging, and knew exactly the right thing to say to me at the right time. I couldn't have done the show without him; I really couldn't. I would not have made it through that many performances. There is so much love and sadness in my heart when I think of him. He made my stepping into the role of Von Gaigernin possible. The director and producer, Tommy Tune, is a very complex thinking man, and being in that production took a lot out of me. Otis not only made it possible, but he also made it comfortable. He passed away not too long after the final performance of *Grand Hotel.* I'll remember him fondly and miss him for the rest of my life. He was one of the great unsung heroes of the theater.

Playing Billy Flynn in the stage musical *Chicago* was a such a blast. Someone asked me if I could have played one of the women in the play, who would it have been. I told them, "I'd have to be Velma because she got to kill two people in the play." In a small-world coincidence, my co-star star from *Dukes*, Tom Wopat, had played the character of Billy Flynn in the play *Chicago* years before. I learned all those words to those songs backwards and forwards. My favorite scene to play in *Chicago* by far was the court room scene, which moves really fast, and there is wonderful slapstick comedy very much like Abbott and Costello. That's my favorite part, in spite of the fact that there is very little singing in that scene, and I love to sing, but it's just so funny. I would just live for that scene.

Hollywood Squirrels

- In those days focus pullers weren't looking at a monitor. They had to depend on the piece of tape on the floor that they had measured during rehearsal. If you were on the tape, then you were in focus. But if you were ahead or behind the tape, he had to adjust accordingly. There's always more to everything than anyone ever thinks.

- It takes years to start a career... minutes to end one. The phone works both ways. Nobody owes you or gives you your next job no matter who you were yesterday. You have to work the system, put yourself out there, and create your own opportunity until it happens again. Regardless of background, social status, color, or education, nobody does anybody any favors. You have to go for it with all your heart and soul all your life. Period.

BEHIND THE SCENES

*"We don't make movies to make money, we
make money to make more movies."*
— *Walt Disney*

When you consider what a success *The Dukes of Hazzard* was, I was fortunate that I didn't fall into what some people might call the television trap. A lot of the great actors in successful television shows at the same time weren't able to break out and do movies for years after their series. Tom Hanks was on the televisions series *Bosom Buddies,* and Robin Williams was still on the *Mork and Mindy* show. So, Hanks and Williams were known for their roles on those shows just like I was known for being Bo Duke. *Dukes of Hazzard* captured America's heart, and I began acting in movies at the same time.

My first movie was *Dream House*, a romantic comedy with Marilu Henner set in New York City. I was delighted that I hadn't been typecast, and Marilu was great to work with. I was literally nineteen years old, and *Dukes* was such a smashing success that the film crew was having to hide me. They kept secretly moving me around from location to location, trying to keep my whereabouts hidden so it wouldn't leak out and draw a crowd. It was just wild, like being Elvis or something. I mean just a few years ago, I was trying out for theater parts in high school, and now I was on a hit television series *and* filming a movie in New York. When I think about it now, it's pretty obvious how popular that little Southern television show with country folks and the General Lee car was for them to have to keep me undercover. Everything was totally surreal and like a dream come true all at once.

The following year I was cast in the lead of the movie *Happy Endings* with Catherine Hicks. In this romantic comedy I played a quirky writer with no Southern accent at all. Those first two movies were pretty lighthearted, but in those early years of *The Dukes*, I also starred in the movies *Cocaine Wars* and *Ministry of Vengeance*. In one I play Miami

DEA agent, Cliff Vickry (After my Great Grandmother), who is working in South America undercover to bring down this notorious drug lord. In *Ministry of Vengeance* I play a Vietnam vet who had a traumatic experience in the war and becomes a minister when he gets out of service. Then his wife and children are killed by terrorists, and he has a serious change of heart and sets out to seek revenge for their deaths. Those characters were tough guys in different ways, and the scripts dealt with some very serious subjects. The roles were a far cry from the smiling, lovable, Southern guy everyone saw on television.

I'd have to say that *Eddie Macon's Run* was my favorite filming experience. Working with Kirk Douglas on that film during a hot Lorado, Texas, summer was amazing. It was also John Goodman's first time in front of the camera. There are enough stories in that experience that I'm going to have to dedicate a chapter in another book to it. Keep your eyes peeled!

I've also had the opportunity to be on screen with some of my greatest heroes. Living legends like Chuck Norris and Johnny Cash. It just doesn't get any better than that. What's truly amazing is when you discover they are the kind of guys who would help you build a fence. That's one of the things I always consider when I meet someone. I want to know if they are the kind of person who would get their hands dirty to help you out if you needed it.

Another guy who was one of the truest, bluest people I ever met in the business was the wrestler Roddy Piper. We were introduced by Vince Gironda, that world-famous body-builder I told you about. He was such a great guy, and we stayed good friends right up until he died a few years ago.

Hollywood being what it is, maybe you don't get to act with some of your favorite people or heroes, and you think, *Wow, I would have loved to have had a chance to work with that guy, but now they've passed and it's too late.* Then you actually end up *playing them* in the movie for their life story. That's exactly what happened to me with Michael Landon.

When I was little, I was a huge *Bonanza* fan. Mom and I would always watch the *Wonderful World of Disney* on Sunday nights. If that wasn't good enough, it was even better when I was allowed to stay up late and watch *Bonanza*. My only problem was there seemed to be no rhyme or reason to when I could stay up late, so watching *Bonanza* wasn't something I could always count on. The nights when I was sent to bed before the show came on, I cracked my bedroom door and stuck a floor length mirror I used for practicing magic in a strategic place so I could see the television from my bed. I actually think my mother knew what I was up to, but she let it slide most Sundays. Like I've said, I always loved Westerns of any kind, but I was also a big fan of Michael Landon. I just couldn't get enough of *Little House on the Prairie, Teenage Werewolf,* and *Highway to Heaven.*

Imagine my surprise the day that I received the call that they wanted me to actually play Michael Landon in a movie. I thought, *I can't play Michael* because he was about 5'9" and a brunette, and I'm over six feet tall, but Les Moonves, who was president of CBS at the time, said, "We want you to do this movie, and Michael's son, Michael Landon Jr., wants you to do it." It was both a great honor to play the role and also challenging for different reasons. I had to read the script that revealed a side of Michael Landon I hadn't known about. Basically, I had to accept that he was a real man and not just an actor I'd loved because of the roles he'd played.

I've never been intimidated by any role, but if one could do it, it would have been acting in the real-life drama about Michael Landon. As if trying to fill those famous shoes wasn't enough, I was also being directed by his son, Michael Landon Jr. That was enough to make me nervous, but, thankfully, I was distracted somewhat by these three different wigs I had to wear during the filming. This isn't the kind of thing you might focus on when you are out promoting a movie, but it's been a few years, so I think it's okay to share a good laugh with you.

There were multiple wigs designed for the role, and we actually had nicknames for the ones that served as the three main wigs. They were the Ponderosa Poodle, the Prairie Poodle, and the Prayer Poodle. There was so much concern about trying to fix the wigs all the time and make them look natural, and any intimidation from the role was out the window with my having to be preoccupied about not looking like a Q-tip on screen. As it turns out, that was all for the best so that I was focusing on the fact that I was playing this television legend. Michael Landon Jr. did a great job directing, and I appreciate his wanting me to play his father.

My dreams of being the cowboy in Westerns who rides in to save the girl finally came to pass when I landed a role in *Dr. Quinn, Medicine Woman.*

Well, almost. I was cast as the character Daniel Simon in an episode called *The Cowboy's Lullaby*. Talking about living a dream! Not only was I in a Western, but also I was playing the guitar, singing, and it looked like my character was a potential love interest to the star. That was, until the character Bryan Sully committed to their relationship. That's okay. I went on to become the sheriff of the town. I didn't end up with the girl, but, hey, I got the badge.

When we were filming *Dr. Quinn*, I would go into my little dressing room and put on my cowboy outfit, and then I'd put on my sheriff badge. Then somebody would knock on the door, and they would hand me my gun after they showed me it was empty, and I'd put it on. Somebody would be coming up to the trailer with the reins to my horse in their hands, and I'd get on the horse with my forty-five on my hip and my sheriff's badge on my leather vest, and I would ride off into the sunset. Well, it was actually toward the set, but for a seven-year-old boy who grew up as a New Yorker only wanting to grow up to be John Wayne, there was no better way to start the day.

I drink a lot of coffee, and the entire time I was playing in *Dr. Quinn*, I drank out of my tin cup that Johnny Cash had given me on the set of *Stagecoach*. Johnny was sometimes a character on the show, and he and June had both been featured guest stars multiple times. The last time I ever saw Johnny Cash alive was right there on the set of *Dr. Quinn, Medicine Woman*.

It was great to be in a long-running series such as *Dukes of Hazzard, Dr. Quinn, and Smallville,* but I also enjoyed guest starring in programs like *Touched by An Angel; Walker, Texas Ranger; CSI; JAG; Glee;* and so many more. Whether you're playing a character on a hit TV series or you're cast as a character for just one episode, it's a good thing to remember that whatever you do that day is going to last a lot longer than you will. Long after I'm gone, people will still be watching all of those television shows and the movies Alicia and I make.

There's never a day that I can just phone it in. It doesn't matter how I feel or if I'm up or down that day, whether it's acting, directing, or writing, I have to keep giving it my all. That goes for paying attention to the details. For instance, something is always evolving, and that means you have to be constantly open to learning new techniques. When we were filming *Smallville,* we started shooting in something called 'letterbox.' That meant we needed to learn to move and stand differently in relation to each other in front of the camera. These small details of movie making are important, and I've never lost my passionate curiosity about the process with this industry that's continuing to change every day.

When you're making movies, you also have to account for 'the unknown factor.' Anything can happen in the movie-making business and often does. When I was making *Smothered,* Roddy Piper was supposed to be in it playing himself, but he came down sick at the last minute and couldn't fly in to play his part. That's when I met Dane Rhodes for the first time. He is an amazing actor who lives in New Orleans and has been in several of our films like *Anderson Bench, Like Son,* and *Inadmissible,* to name a few. He stepped in with less than a week's notice and knocked it out of the park. He's the guy who burns up in the RV in *Smothered.* I asked him if he could recite any Shakespeare from memory, and, of course, he could. So that's what I had him doing in the movie because he felt like a "real" actor stuck in the stigma of a horror-film guy. You'll see all the references to the John Carpenter movie, *They Live,* that Roddy did. If you wonder why those are there... now you know.

Writing has been another part of the storytelling process that captivates me. Some of the scripts I've written are darker in nature, but they're also funny. I enjoyed writing a horror movie where the girl who is normally the victim turns out to actually be the killer. I remember watching horror movies growing up, and it thrilled me as a kid. You know, the kind of movie where you're watching, knowing you are safe and sound at home, but something happens and you suddenly almost jump right out of your skin. I just loved that feeling!

In *Smothered,* a group of horror icons are having a terrible thriller convention, and they aren't making any money. Out of the blue they get offered this job to go haunt an RV Park for the weekend, (not trailer park because, according to the character Agness, "Trailer Parks are for trash.") Being down and out, they immediately accept it. What they don't know is it's a set-up, and the girl who hired them is about to kill them off one by one. Instead of having these beautiful girls getting terrorized by some guy in a mask, you have these guys in masks getting terrorized by this beautiful girl. A strange but fun twist on the old horror genre. It was a blast to film. It has a 'who's who' of the horror genre actors, and they came together to be in a movie for the first time. My whole point in the making of it was to get people to laugh and jump out of their skins, to feel like I had as a kid, and I think we succeeded at that.

4:Go is another one of our thriller movies about four escaped convicts who think they've gotten away with murder, but they have actually been lured into four different horrible, delightful traps. We had some great people in the cast: Dean Cain, who played the Superman character on *Lois and Clark,* Cary Cayhill from *The Walking Dead,* and Marcus 'Buff' Bagwell as well. It's a dark movie; I admit that, but there are a lot of people who enjoy horror movies and dark thrillers with a touch of comedy to them.

Alicia and I both like to evoke emotions and take a genre and turn it upside down. We love to shoot things that are puzzles and to entertain people by leading them astray so that they don't see what's coming next. We want them to laugh and gasp at almost the same time. Trying to do that type of thing with a studio is little more difficult for something that's unique or different from the known genre model. Because of Alicia's production savvy, I realized you don't have to spend a bunch of money to make a movie. You can spend less money more wisely, as long as you're telling a good story and the characters are fleshed out on the page. I always thought you had to have the blessing of studio executives, but now I realize they might have a different vision or dream they are ultimately pursuing. I'm so happy that we can get that vision fleshed out and on film for pennies on the dollar. Because of that we don't have to go to a group of people like studio people or to have their blessing. We get to work independently doing what we love to entertain people. We do what we want to do next based on our schedule and also in a unique way based on the people who show up in our lives. We'll meet someone we like and say, "Oh, my gosh, that's such a great person for that character we were thinking of. Let's make that movie next."

Whether we're shooting a love story or a murder mystery, we love to invert it and do something a little different. We're not hinging on whether or not we get a thumbs-up or thumbs-down; we're still going to make movies because we enjoy it so much. You're destined to fail when all of your concentration is in trying to create something to impress someone else. You have to create what excites you whether it's movies or towels, soap, or dental implants. And sometimes that means you have to figure out a way to do it independently. Don't get me wrong; there's nothing at all wrong with the studio system. I understand it has to be the way it is. It's a kind of corporate creativity mentality. I don't fault it at all. I mean, just look at all those John Wayne movies I grew up watching and loving. John Wayne had a hard time getting *The Alamo* movie done, so he paid for it himself and risked everything to do it. Lost everything, too! No one wanted to back his little patriotic movie. It's funny looking back on that now, but it just didn't have corporate studio support at the time. Alicia and I realized we're not corporate personalities.

For instance, *Anderson Bench* was going in one direction when I wrote it, but when we started casting it, it went in another direction. Being independent movie makers, we don't have to ask permission to make those changes during the process. We also don't have to appeal to a large group to see if it's okay to film in Louisiana, change a scene, or cast a particular person. Not having to ask permission on those kinds of things not only saves a lot of time, it also saves a lot of money. I believe that money should go on the screen.

We've been most surprised and honored that there are people of such high caliber who have been in our films and are willing to work for so little on the chance that the films will succeed. In that way they know that the way we operate, they'll get something on the back end. The quality of actors who have been willing to be in our movies, to invest in us with their time and talent moves us deeply. We can't wait until the day comes that Alicia can cook an amazing dinner, and we can all be together and surprise them with a check for playing their part. We have a great crew of people across the board willing to come to work for a hundred dollars a day. People keep showing up and taking a chance, rolling the creative dice with us, time after time. We've now developed a family of film-makers. We have the actors who continue to participate in our movies, and they'll play distinctly different characters in each film. They are bringing a lot to the table and at the same time having a chance to show their diversity.

We also let people have quite a bit of creative freedom, and that endears the process to them. When we were filming *Anderson Bench,* Duke Davis Roberts played the owner of a drive-through liquor store. For people who may not know what those are, they are a real thing where we live. When he asked for my direction I said, "I want you to do whatever you want. I want you to do whatever no one else in their right mind would let you do." That's when he came up with that odd martial arts dance he was doing at the drive-through liquor store in *Anderson Bench.* He had a blast playing that role.

To keep the budget to a minimum we also do absolutely everything we can when we're making the movies. We build sets; we costume; we do it all. We just go for it. It's hard to stop something once you've started, so we always make sure we have a starting point and just jump right in there. It also helps budget wise for the producer, director, actors, writers – everyone – to all be on the same page. Everyone needs to know that they are making the same movie. Adversity is expensive. No time on a set for debate.

Our next project is something exciting and a complete turn-around from those horror and thriller genres we've been making. I've just written the script for a new movie, *Christmas Cars.* We're already having a great time thinking about casting in advance, and this is one that I will be starring in. The movie is my answer to a lot of questions for the fans of *Dukes of Hazzard.* It lets people know that *Dukes* wasn't just about car chases down dirt roads, Daisy-Duke shorts, and cute talk. No successful recipe like *Dukes* is just one thing. It has to have a lot of ingredients in it. It has to have a lot of love and integrity. I've paid close attention for forty years to what people have shared with me that they loved most about *Dukes of Hazzard.* I've written this script thinking about all of those things. It's a family movie that everyone will love, and we can't wait to begin filming what we know is going to be an instant classic for *Dukes* fans.

Making stories people love so much that they outlast a lifetime. That has to be one of the greatest magic acts of all.

Movie Trick Squirrel

- You aren't aware of all of the edit points, different shots and angles, in a movie or television show because the sound hides it. If you want to make yourself aware of all this then watch an episode with the sound turned way down or, better yet, off altogether. Suddenly you'll understand the number of angles and camera setups that go into an hour (42 minutes, actually) of television.

HOW DO YOU STOP THE WATER?

"You can't let a little thing like a national
disaster destroy your dream."
— *John R. Schneider*

Camp Singing Waters was a church camp on fifty-eight acres in Holden, Louisiana, a small town between New Orleans and Baton Rouge. I was looking for a place to film a movie, and the owner kept after me to take a look. To appease him, I finally stopped by on my way to the airport. That's when it happened.

There's a special feeling to this land, and the moment I stepped on it, I fell in love with it. I started walking around looking at everything, and the movie I wanted to produce just started coming to life in my mind. There was this incredible five-acre bamboo forest, a baseball field, a big, old lake, and a hundred-year-old house on the grounds. It was situated in a bend with the Tickfaw River on both sides. It was the perfect place to not only live but also be able to make movies. I told the man that afternoon, "Yes, this is it. This is the place."

My dream has always been to continue making movies, and at Camp Singing Waters you could take your camera and turn it in every direction and see something different. It was a perfect setting for filming independent movies on a budget. Transferring all of your equipment to different locations, paying for housing for your actors and crew and all that is extremely expensive, so when you're able to stay in one place and have such variety with endless possibilities, well, that's something you just can't easily recreate or find somewhere else.

I've always found water to be a very calming influence. Being on Lake Sunapee at acting camp. Getting out there on Old Hickory Lake with Johnny Cash. Those were some of my best memories I've ever had. Just watching the wind pick up and blow across the surface gives your soul a chance to settle down a little bit and lets your mind calm down from all your troubles.

But water's got another side to it, and that's an ugly, dangerous side I don't wish on anybody. That's the side when the rains come and keep on coming. That's when water doesn't care who you are, where you've been, or what your plans are. Water goes where it wants to, and where it has to, and like it or not, it'll take you with it.

In 2016 the rains started, and it seemed they never stopped. It rained on us every day. I remembered it coming down like that at my Great-grandma Vickrey's place in Florida. And here, in Louisiana, when the rains started, we watched the skies open up, and we watched the waterline rise higher every day. We'd take the dogs and walk down to the water's edge, and we'd see where it had covered up another one of those old cypress roots that stood up out of the ground. Inch by inch, they disappeared under the rising water. Friends and family started calling, asking about us, and we'd tell them, "We're keeping an eye on it, but it sure seems to be coming up fast."

In the middle of everything we had our dogs, Stormy and Gumbo, with us, and knew they were safe and sound. Our other two, Gravy and Duke, were allowed to run the property at will, and that's when they went missing. We called and called and went searching for them but couldn't find them anywhere. I was fearing the worst, and everybody we knew was out in boats looking for them. When I had first laid eyes on it lazily rambling by the house, the Tickfaw was one of the most peaceful sights I'd ever seen, but when the dogs went missing, the Tickfaw wasn't running past the house, it was running through it. We thought we'd lost them for certain, but they had managed to get up on one of the porches of a building we used for a set sometimes, so they were safe. That was a real happy moment standing there in the middle of so much destruction.

The house we lived in was also part of a set, and even though it was a film set, it was also where I kept so many things that were near and dear to me. I had photos of Mom when she was a little girl in Sanford, Florida, family mementos like that are just irreplaceable. The flood water came up in the house, and every closet, cabinet, and drawer was full of water.

Flood waters can be dangerous for so many reasons, one of them being that they can carry you away, but the other is what they leave behind. When they rush in, they are full of all kinds of stuff like oil and sewage run-off, but if that's not bad enough, the house started growing mold, which, as we now know, can kill you.

We were out there wading through all that nastiness and doing our best to try to salvage what we could. The cars we had on set used to be way in the back of the house, but the water just carried them up and dumped them in the front. It turned our world upside down. Nothing was where it was supposed to be.

I tried to look at it like, *Hey we're alive; the dogs are alive, so that's the main thing, and it's just given me a chance to get rid of a lot of things I needed to get rid of anyway.* That was my way of trying to make myself feel better. You know, just saying, *Oh, I had too much clutter anyway.* But the truth is, it ruined things that I had wanted to keep for my great-great-great grandchildren to have, things I wanted them to be able to pass down generation to generation. Here they were lying out everywhere on tables and they were soaking wet. Alicia was trying to take pictures and photograph Mom's memories the best she could to save them because our next step was we had no choice but to burn them.

Before the floods came, we used to have concerts in the barn, and we also had a little Shakespeare festival, but everything in the barn, every light, every microphone, every piece of electronics, every wire, was destroyed. The water current came through the barn so strong that it took picnic tables from hundreds of yards away and swept them into the barn, lifted up the stage and shoved them up under it. There were all these things that showed up that we had never seen. There were couches, hot water heaters, and refrigerators. There were car parts and things we couldn't identify. We still find things today that we have no idea where they came from. A bunch of our stuff washed away, and we still can't ever find it. If you happen to find an old hot tub in your yard, it just might be mine. I can't tell you how much sand washed in from the Tickfaw. We used to have a baseball field, but that has turned into a beach.

I went on Facebook right after the flood and asked anyone who could help to please come pitch in because at that point the churches in the area were just overwhelmed with need. There was a lot of destruction, but not enough hands to clean it up. Then people started coming in from states away. You can't count on the weather; you can't count on the things you own, but you can count on people who will come to help you in your time of need. Folks came from Texas, Mississippi, Alabama, and Florida. People came from everywhere. And they kept on coming. Not only that, local people showed up while their own houses were still flooded and under water. The people of Louisiana looked at it with just the most down-to-earth attitude and said, "Well, this is what happened. Now, we got to get to work. My house is still under water, so let me see what I can do to help somebody else out until the water gets out of my kitchen. Then maybe someone will come help me."

When people ask me, "How do you think God works?" I can honestly tell them, "God sends people. People who care. He'll give you the supplies and tools to build someone else's house. He'll give somebody else the supplies and tools to build yours."

Those people showed up from everywhere, and they were a gift to us. They came out with their little fishing boats on trailers behind their trucks so they could rescue people or help clean up. People started calling them the Cajun Navy.

I kept posting live Facebook feeds all during the flood, and people were tuning in to watch because there just wasn't a lot of television coverage. For one thing, it wasn't a hurricane, so it didn't have a name. That seems like a minor thing, but when the media is reporting about a storm, it's the name of the storm that becomes the star. People kept checking the posts because otherwise they didn't know what was happening. Even the facts about the lay of the land were confusing because people not familiar with Louisiana think the entire state is under sea level, but that's not true at all. Actually, very little of Louisiana is under sea level.

Out of that tragedy some good things happened. Alicia and I had started working together to make movies, and we had started dating. The only thing that got me through that time was Alicia. Without a doubt, those floods brought us closer together.

It was such a moving experience not only because of what I had lost but also for what I witnessed all around me, and because of that, I started singing songs about the experience. Those songs were stories about what I had lived through and about the tragedy I experienced firsthand. They paint the dark part of that experience in words, but they also show this great spirit of resilience of the people of Louisiana that resulted in the face of such adversity.

Ruffled Skirts, the album title, is the reference to the skirts on the trailers that were ruffled when the flood waters came through. Just take a look at that album cover and see if it doesn't pull at your heart. "How Do You Stop the Water" is such a heartfelt piece of my life, so I'm very, very proud of that. The band is listed as *John Schneider and the Cajun Navy*. I thought that would be the perfect salute to those people who showed up to help.

There are also some fun songs on the album like "Down in Louisiana We're All Going With the Flow," which is a party song. There's a good reason for that because when a storm hits, there's always someone who decides, *Okay we don't have any electricity; all the food we have is going to spoil; all our beer is gonna get hot. Let's find some dry charcoal and light it up and put everything we have on the grill and get all of us together, even if we have to set up on the roof!*

In the middle of all that devastation I knew it was important for me not to give up. A dream is a hard thing to carry sometimes, but you must. You can't let a little thing like a national disaster destroy your dream. If that's all it took for me to give up on my dream, then it wasn't much of a dream to start with. You always have to do the very best that you can with where you're standing.

Flood Squirrel

- One of things that needs to be done is cleaning out all the debris that washed into the Tickfaw. We haven't been able to do that because it's against the state law to dredge the river. But part of the work is making certain that the waters can run their natural course, that they have the ability to follow the natural flow of the river and not be obstructed. That's something we have to work on as local citizens and the time to do that is now before another flood finds us.

THE NEXT BIG THING

"You did not just say that!"
— Tyler Perry

I thank God every day for *The Haves and the Have Nots*. Working with Tyler Perry on the Oprah Winfrey Network is an amazing experience as an actor, but it's also been an incredible place to learn new things in so many ways. I told both Tyler and Oprah that I wasn't ready to learn anything after I turned fifty. I didn't think I had anything else I needed to learn because I was still working on the lessons I was going through. They've both shown me that I was wrong about that because there are new ways of putting your creativity to work.

Tyler Perry and Oprah Winfrey both have a degree of focus and passion for the work they do that's exceptional. I first met Oprah when she was a talk show host in Chicago, and I was promoting the movie *Eddie Macon's Run*. I've never met anyone who was so prepared ahead of time. She really knew her stuff. When Oprah became the person we know today with her OWN network, it never surprised me. Also, she makes you feel like a million bucks when you meet her in person, regardless of who you are.

The Haves and Have the Nots is about three families: a young family who one would say is the have nots; the Harringtons, who are a part of the haves; and the Cryer family who also are part of the haves. It shows you the trials of people no matter where they are in life. Up or down, rich or poor. It showcases the fact that just because you're rich and powerful doesn't mean that you are without heartaches or have more happiness.

They contacted me and invited me to audition and sent me a script. When I first read *The Haves and Have the Nots,* it struck me immediately, *This is the next big thing.* I had that same feeling that I had when I read *Dukes of Hazzard* and *Smallville. This is it, I thought. Where have you been, old friend?*

They told me they were meeting people at the Sheraton hotel on Sunset

Boulvard across from the House of Blues. When I went in, there were a lot of people. I had never met Tyler Perry, but I could see immediately there was something different about him. They had invited five or so people in to audition for each of the roles. He had everyone read in different pairings, this person read with that person, and then read with someone else. I realized he was casting chemistry like they had in *Dukes*. Tyler did several months of work in that same afternoon by getting all these people together in a conference room and saying, "Go for it." So, this casting is more like *America's Got Talent*. You'd think it might make you uncomfortable, but it did the opposite; it helped you relax. You're hanging out with all of these people waiting to be called in to read with someone, and some of them you haven't seen in years, and it turns into just a wonderful, friendly experience.

I remember the night I heard I'd gotten the role of Jim Cryer. I was in Louisiana, on Marvin Henderson's porch, actually, in the middle of talking on the phone with actress Meg Ryan. I was down there scouting out a location for a movie I wanted to make called *Backwater*. Meg had read it and wanted to play the role, and I was talking to her about it, and my agent rang through. I told her I had to call her right back. I hung up and called my agent, and he said, "Congratulations, you got the part on *The Haves and Have the Nots*," which was just great news. I called Meg Ryan right back and we kept talking about *Backwater*.

Tyler Perry has created a character that makes JR Ewing look like a choir boy. Larry Hagman is just the nicest guy in the world when you meet him. You would never in the world believe he wasn't that guy, but he wasn't. He just loved playing that character like I love playing Jim Cryer.

Tyler is always telling me, "Whatever you do, just don't smile." We shoot an hour show every single day during season, so it has a very immediate feel to it. Even on *Dallas*, they took an entire week to film an episode. But that kind of production being possible is all due to Tyler Perry's being one of the most focused, efficient people I've ever worked with. Tyler Perry has shown me how efficiently you can shoot a series or a movie. I imagine when some people first heard about this little show, they didn't give it much thought. I knew better. I knew it was something special, but I still had no idea that the show was going to be such a huge hit. It's the number-one show for Tuesday nights.

I'm a naturally sarcastic person anyway, and sometimes we'll be shooting, and from the other room, I'll hear Tyler say, "You did not just say that!" And I'll say, "Yes, I did." Then he'll say, "Good, say it again." So ad-libbing is okay. I come from a long line of sarcastic men, and inevitably something will just come out of my mouth, and then I'll hear Tyler from behind the wall say, "Put the knife down, Jim." Every time I'm in a scene with Catherine, if there's a knife in the room, I seem to pick it up. Tyler will say, "We're just acting here, guys, remember? Don't pick up the knife."

Working with Tika Sumpter is fantastic. I actually feel that Jim Cryer loves Candace, the character Tika plays, because I believe he has met his match in her. When you've met your match everything becomes most interesting. Tyler has said those two characters are like two snakes battling each other. The chemistry of the two of us on stage has been what Tyler refers to as 'electric.' He credits much of the popularity of the show with people being addicted to finding out what happens next between these two people.

The funny thing is, if you see an interview with some actors from the show, we all slide right into being those characters instead of actually being ourselves. Jim Cryer has a different kind of chemistry happening with Angela Robinson's character. We were on a radio interview for 103.9 New York, which was also taped in the studio. Tyler should have been filming the entire thing. Our conversation, our body language, everything going on between us was exactly like the characters were in front of the camera, and it was very emotionally charged. The host said she needed to bring in popcorn and watch. I think maybe she was trying to crack a joke and defuse the situation just a little bit and get us to laugh.

Jim Cryer's character eventually devolves as the series continues, and that has made it so much more interesting for me as an actor. He starts out on top of the world as a very wealthy powerful judge in Savannah, Georgia, with a wife who ignores him. He is the only character I've known since J.R. Ewing who could be in jail and still feel that he is the master of his own destiny, so I'm loving every moment of it. When somebody who was very powerful gets down and then crawls back out from the underbrush, he does it with a vengeance. It has a lot to do with coming to grips with the fact that you can't control everything. I think one of the reasons that viewers are loving the show so much is that not only is it blockbuster entertainment, but also, we never know what to expect next. The series is full of surprises, and people watching can sense that.

The Haves and the Have Nots is a show that a lot of people schedule to watch together like they did *The Dukes of Hazzard*. I have guys coming up to me all the time saying, "I didn't want to watch that show at all, and my wife made me start watching it with her." When I ask them, "How's that working out for you?" They tell me they can't stop and that they are completely hooked.

FINDING MY SMILE

"Every day brings a chance for you to draw in
a breath, kick off your shoes, and dance."
– Oprah Winfrey

One of my greatest surprises in life occurred years ago when I was in London, England, and I received an emergency notice from the front desk.

Marie Osmond has called and says it's urgent. You have to call her back right away.

I have known Marie since we did the People's Choice awards in 1980, and we are great friends. But getting a phone call from her wasn't part of our everyday relationship. Getting an emergency call when I was out of the country meant something absolutely horrendous had happened. I returned the call right away and was expecting horrible news, but she casually started the conversation by asking me how I was doing and making small talk. Then she dropped the bombshell on me.

"Donnie has injured himself jumping off the piano, and I would love for you to fly in, take over for him and do the show."

"Show? What show?" I asked her.

"The Vegas show," she said.

"There's no way," I told her. "I'm not a dancer. I can't do that."

But she assured me it was okay. She told me they'd design the show around me so I wouldn't have to do all the dancing numbers and that I could sing some of my music, so I'd already be familiar with it. Finally, I agreed.

"Okay, okay, I'll do it. When do you need me?"

"Monday," she said.

This was Friday, and, again, I was still in London. They rushed the music to me, and I remember learning the lines on the plane. I flew into Las Vegas on Sunday. I thought we were going to have a lot of rehearsals like we had for the Broadway shows, but there wasn't a rehearsal scheduled until Monday afternoon. I went on stage Monday night performing and dancing at the Flamingo Hotel in Las Vegas with just a few hours to rehearse.

If just flying in from England with no rehearsal time wasn't difficult enough, they had these little earpiece monitors instead of the large stage ones I was used to. I could hear the music in the earpiece that I was supposed to be singing to, but I could also hear a track of Donnie giving himself notes on what foot to start with, and what step to take next. It was crazy! After that wild experience, if you'd have asked me if I would ever get up in front of a world-wide audience competing in a dance competition, I'd have laughed in your face and said, "Not a chance!"

Dancing With the Stars was a challenge like no other. I was the oldest competitor that year, so let that inspire you to try new things at every age. I had to miss one of the final rehearsals for the first week because I was performing at the Grand Ole Opry, but thankfully, my dance partner, Emma Slater, was a huge fan of the Opry, so she totally understood.

Every week we had to perform a different type of dance, and each one of them presented a different set of challenges. I was nervous about all of it, and I wanted to please Emma, who was working so hard to help me pick up the choreography and not make a thousand mistakes. I knew it was a competition and that scores are everything, but I also had to try not to focus on that entirely. I learned that dancing in many ways was like making movies or writing songs. It was about telling the story, entertaining people, and connecting with the audience. That helped me relax and play to the crowd.

One of the most fun dances to perform was when we danced to the song "I Want To Be Like You" from Disney's movie, *The Jungle Book*. It had always been one of my favorite songs. It brought back those Sunday nights I'd watched the *Wonderful World of Disney* with Mom, and she'd heard me walk around the house singing that song with gusto. I was so proud when judge Bruno Tonioli said that I'd really brought some "sparkle to the jungle." I had been the most worried about us having to do the Quickstep, but it ended up being some of the highest scores we received.

I was also starring in the *The Haves and the Have Nots,* where people were used to seeing me show up every Tuesday night as this horrible character, and then they see me up there smiling and dancing under the lights. I think they were completely shocked. "Jim Cryer is smiling and doing the tango? What in the world is happening?"

Although all of the dances were challenging in different ways, nothing was more of a challenge than the night that *Dancing With The Stars* featured a film clip of me talking about all of the tough things that I was going through. Emma and I were told just before the show that we were going to watch the part in which I talked about my divorce, my estrangement from my children, and about mom dying. Then I told her about Alicia and how we'd started dating and how when my mom saw us together, she said, "John, you've found your smile."

All week Emma and I had rehearsed a very special dance to the song "Smile" and planned to dedicate it to my mom, but after watching that clip, I wondered if I'd be able to move at all, much less be able to make it all the way through the dance. Emma was worried I was going to forget the steps. There was no number of rehearsals that could have prepared me for the depth of emotion I felt after watching that video. We were standing backstage ready to go on, and Emma could see that I was trying to hold it together. She turned to me and said, "Even though we're dedicating this to your mom, when we finish this dance, I want you to be in that better place in 2016. I want you to be exactly where you were when you found your smile."

At the end of that dance, when Emma released me, it was as if Mom had released me, knowing it was okay for her to leave me, and that I finally had someone who loved me as much as she did. I ended the dance with my arms up in the lights, flower petals falling all around me, wearing that smile.

If I'd have gone home that night after dancing to "Smile," I would have been able to go to Alicia and say, "Thank God, you made this possible. It was one of the best nights of my life." Of all the years I've been in show business, it was the first time in my life that I can honestly say that I felt truly elegant. No... even better. I felt something I had never felt before. I felt graceful.

It was so great to see a company like *Dancing with the Stars* that pay attention to things that are so human and so hurtful and treat them with a delicate touch. Even though we didn't win the finale, I was able to continue competing for seven weeks. Then I had the wonderful opportunity to go back for finale night and debut one of my new songs, *Walk a Mile in My Shoes.*

Las Vegas Squirrel

- I have this recurring dream that someone calls me at the last minute to do a show like Grand Hotel or The Music Man or Fiddler on the Roof to fill in for the lead who just got into an accident and can't make curtain. In this dream I always say "Okay… I'll do it." I show up and realize just as I'm about to make my entrance that I don't have a clue what to do once I get on stage! As I was waiting for the elevator to raise me up for my first song at The Flamingo with Marie, I was 90% sure that this was actually that dream! The elevator came up, and I saw the crowd and started to sing. I swear it wasn't until halfway through the first show that I was convinced that this was actually happening and not that damn dream.

THIS AIN'T EASY STREET

*"Going in one more round when you don't think you can.
That's what makes all the difference in your life."*
— *Rocky Balboa*

I've gone through some tough times. I won't lie. When people see some of the things I've done or the fact I was in the hit television series *Dukes of Hazzard* when I was only eighteen, it might look like it all came easy or that I had things handed to me. Nothing could be further from the truth. In the early days when I was first starting my career in television, I felt like the pirate in the *Pirates of the Caribbean,* with one foot on the dock and one on the boat. I was singing and being cast in movies. The television show was a hit, but I kept thinking one of them would surely catch fire at any moment and disappear, and then I'd be like that pirate, and I'd have to hurry to jump into the one that wasn't burning to survive. That might have been a holdover from growing up being very aware of the financial struggles we were going through. In some ways, I was still that kid with the shoeshine box, trying to get hired to do magic tricks, play guitar, or be in a play. In a very real way I'm still using my dad's philosophy of having something to fall back on. When something starts to slow or falter, I'm always ready to move over to something else. Not something new. Something old and comfortable and familiar like my *Dukes* boots. It's been working for over forty years. Thanks, dad!

My parents divorced when I was only two years old. My older brother, Bob went to live with my dad, but I was basically still a baby, only two years old, and I stayed with my mom. My parents had their reasons for doing things the way they did. No matter what I thought about it as a kid, since then life has taken me down some dark roads and turns I never saw coming, now I can honestly say, maybe they were doing the best they could. Maybe they were just trying to figure things out and get by one day at a time.

One of the things that I'm so appreciative of looking back is that in spite of the fact that our parents were divorced, Bob and I have a great relationship. Don't get me wrong; he and my step-brother, Mark, were older and used to terrorize me as a kid. It happens. We weren't raised together, but now that we are past the halfway mark, it seems as if we've always been side by side. He's the mayor of a beautiful village in New York state, Stamford, and always has time to call and ask how we're doing. Thinking back on it, it seems he's always been one of my greatest supporters, which I so appreciate. I was happy to gain another bonus, my brother, Mark, when Dad remarried. So, it is true what they say that good things can come out of bad times.

You know when you're little your parents seem so old and tall at the time. You think at that age they should know all the answers, but the truth is, they don't. None of us has or ever will. But we do the very best with what we have to work with every day. And we try to remember to be kind to one another along the way. To treasure our family and friends and hang onto the people who have had an impact on our lives for good. I have been really blessed with some of both, but I have also valued good, old, hard work. Using my own wits and muscles were part of my life at a very young age.

For a while, what felt like an eternity at that age, Mom and I lived in the basement of Grandma and Grandpa Dugan's house. As much as I loved them, I sure didn't love the basement. When I say we lived there, I mean a basement that was dark and cut out of the rock of a wall like something from *The Great Escape* prison movie. Not at all like some nice, finished-out basement turned into a nice apartment. For a while, Mom and I even lived in some little twelve-by-twelve room that used to be some post office or something. That wasn't very cushy either.

So, I have never just had anything handed to me financially. I learned to respect hard work at a young age. To this day, Kiwi Shoe Polish smells like a quarter to me. Having that experience of working hard, of respecting a dollar, and knowing how much sweat it took to earn it is an element I think I've brought into the characters I've played. Those are qualities that you don't unlearn or easily forget. When times are tough, you push up your sleeves and get in there and look for a job. Then you do whatever job you find, whether it's bussing tables, digging a ditch, or being in front of a movie camera, you do it with all your heart. You go to work when you're sick and don't feel good. You try to figure out a way to make something happen when you don't know how you're going to survive the next thirty days.

After being a kid who suffered through my parents getting a divorce, I ended up going through that same story more than once. Tawny and I divorced after three years of marriage. I then married Elly Castle in 1993, happily adopted Chasen and Leah (her children from a previous marriage and who I consider my own), and then we had Karis in 1996. Divorce is not something you'd wish on your worst enemy. I have been going through a divorce for over four years. It's been the kind of awful that bad fairy tales are made of. It seems every day it just gets more like you are drowning in some kind of quicksand.

If I could give a word of advice to any person out there reading this who is headed for divorce, I mean when you know that's where the road is going and there is no turning this car around, then I would say to do it in the most civil and cheapest way you can. Don't go out and immediately hire a bunch of lawyers and decide you're going to go to court to get some kind of justice, because in my experience, justice was not what was waiting at the end of the line. It was jail. In the end, it cost me hundreds of thousands of dollars I didn't have and had to borrow, and still nothing was settled. And it cost my ex-wife everything she had too. It just got ridiculous, and I don't think either of us 'won,' but we both lost a lot of time and money.

Things happen; people change, and the best you can hope for is that life goes on and you can just hang onto your health and the people you love. The very worst part about the divorce for me has been that it's wedged itself in between me and my three adult children. And now I'm at the point of realizing that there is nothing I can do except hope one day one of my kids will call me or show up to just say "Hi, Dad."

I imagine that many of the people reading this have gone through some troubled times in their lives. Whether it's a flood or a divorce or whatever it may be that comes against you to knock you off your feet, you have to do the best you can to get back up again. It's like Rocky Balboa said, "It ain't about how hard you can hit. It's about how hard you can get hit and keep moving forward." Thanks, Sly!

This can sure be a bittersweet life we're living, but it's like I've said about country music being made up of three chords and the truth. Like music, life can shine a light on things that are wonderful or not so wonderful. And sometimes things are even worse than we ever imagined they would be. Sometimes, they are downright heart-wrenching.

Perception can be a key player in the story. People can see you doing something or on an interview or being up on stage at a concert, and it looks like you are rolling in money and living a rock star lifestyle when really you're just, you know, eating beans out of a can at the end of the day and trying to keep the lights turned on. I know you know what I'm talking about. The neighbors may say a lot of things about you, or the press may say a lot of things because of what they perceive is the truth when it isn't. They don't know when you close the door at the end of the day what burdens you're actually carrying and what's really going on in your life. They don't know that you're getting up early so you can juggle balls of fire like some magic act to keep the show rolling. And, that's okay. They aren't supposed to know because it's your job to go out there and make it look easy. To punch that clock with a smile on your face, or maybe, it's to teach another class with your shoulders back so the students don't suspect a thing. Whatever it is that you do in life, nobody knows what it's like to walk in your shoes and carry that load but you and God. I understand that because I'm the same way. Trust me, I'm right there with you. I've been down and out. And I've been open and honest about it. One of my favorite lines in *Christmas Cars* is "Welcome to the lifestyles of the broke and famous." I love it 'cause I've lived it.

I've lost my land and been through a divorce and was locked up because I didn't have the nineteen thousand a month they wanted me to pay. Most people don't live their lives in front of the camera, but it's what I'm called to do. So, I keep showing up. But I won't deny the truth that there are days it ain't Easy Street. That's the best way to say it. And to be honest, it never was. Sure, I had some times that seemed like a whole lot of years of hard work had paid off. Some years where I had money like when I was able to bless my mom for being there for me and to relieve some of the struggles she had gone through all of my life. Those were good days and good years. But

I've also seen my share of struggles back then like I do now. And nothing has been more painful than losing my relationship with my kids.

I keep hoping that one day there will be a knock at the door, and when I go to open it, they'll be standing there. Or that I'll just look out in the audience at a concert, and one of them will have shown up to surprise me. Every Monday night when I was filming *Dancing With the Stars,* I'd look out at the crowd, every single week, and think maybe tonight, maybe this will be the night it'll happen.

There can be a lot of condemnation and judgment out there from people who don't even know me or just hear something unkind that passes though some grapevine or on the Internet. Maybe they hear a snatch of a story that doesn't tell the whole picture at all. It's like playing that old game we used to play as kids where everyone would sit in the circle and someone would whisper something to the person next to them, and then they'd pass it on, and they'd repeat it to the person on the other side of them. It gets repeated and repeated, over and over again, until at the end of the circle when someone says what they heard aloud, it doesn't sound anything at all like it started out.

That's what the years of the divorce have been like. It's where you just wonder, *My God, what was that all about?* What a huge waste of money no one had and more than that a waste of energy, of years of your life you can't get back that you had to spend on that. I'd rather have spent all that time focused on the good things. I'd rather choose to remember the good times. I try to do that with my childhood and with the years since then, no matter what I've encountered.

But I can tell you this right now. I wouldn't take anything for the years I had with my kids and watching them grow up. Being their father gave me some of the greatest years of my life. Like experiencing Christmas with them when they were little kids and shopping for them and being about as excited about every little thing as they were. Man, what a joy that was.

It's all about being there during those different stages in life. And I was able to be there in a big way. Like I said, I made sure I was commuting back and forth every week while filming *Smallville* for those five years because I didn't want to miss anything. I didn't want to miss being there for them if they needed me, but it was also because I needed them. I missed them when I was away from them, and I didn't want to miss being a part of their everyday lives, to hear what went on in school that day or who was their new best friend or just to watch their favorite television shows with them.

Now, when people bring up my role on *Smallville* what I immediately think of is Leah, Chasen, and Karis, because to me those five years I was on the show was really all about them. Those were their years. Here I was playing Superman's dad, one of the most iconic roles of a lifetime, but my most important role to me was being their dad. They were still in those early years, and those ages where everything is new, and every year brings new changes. Being a part of their lives and watching them grow up were some of the best years of my life. It's the kind of thing when young parents are dreaming of how much they'd like to have a baby, and they're looking forward to watching them grow up. I got to experience that in life, and that's a real blessing. I don't take any of those years for granted. Not a single one. I'm so thankful for them.

If I could say anything to them now it would be to just tell them how much I love them, and that no matter what they hear or anyone says to them, or what it looks like in this crazy world, that I will always be their dad. And that wherever I am, they'll always have a place they can call home. That day or night, the door to the house is going to be as wide open to them as the door to my heart is.

WE ALL NEED A MIRACLE

"I had those dark memories of Grassland
I carried around with me everywhere."
— John R. Schneider

People always want to ask me about the Children's Miracle Network Hospitals, and I sure can understand why. It's something worth bragging about not because of my being a co-founder but because it's been going strong for over thirty-six years now. We've raised almost eight billion dollars for children's hospitals, and most of that has been by people donating one dollar at a time.

Three things in my life influenced me to try to fix the problems that I saw when it came to charities dedicated to helping sick children. When I was little, I was the fat, wheezing kid with an asthma inhaler. Back in the 1960s, where I grew up, when I had to go somewhere for testing, I ended up in a place called Grassland, where they tested me for tuberculosis. It sounds like a place where they send old cows to die, and it was just awful. They had all these sick adults dying of emphysema just parked out there in the hallway. There were terrible things that I saw on every trip. I never was admitted overnight, but I was there a lot getting tested, and it was scary.

My dad had been in a square dance band, and every year they had a special dance for people in wheelchairs. Seeing these people had a profound effect on me that's lasted all through these years. I could see how much this special event meant to them. It was obvious to me how much they appreciated someone spending time focused on making their lives better.

Then, in Atlanta, when I was seventeen, Martha Eddins had a theater group, and we would perform at the children's hospitals during Christmas and Thanksgiving. We'd do part of a show like *The Music Man* or *Wizard of Oz* for all the kids there. Seeing these kids in wheelchairs, with all these tubes and wires hanging out of them, singing along or trying to dance to a tune. Wow! Those images stayed in my mind. I never forgot those children or the fact that they were fighting for their very lives. Talk about courage. These kids were worth every minute of the time I spent there entertaining them, and even at that age I knew that.

Flash forward a few years and I was the entertainment chairman for March of Dimes. I was dedicated to the telethon, but I wanted to address some issues that were important to me about the best way we could serve all those sick children I remembered performing for in Atlanta. Searching for answers to those issues initiated discussions that very soon led to the creation of the Children's Miracle Network.

My brother, Bob, still talks about how he can't just get over me being so focused on getting the Children's Miracle Network off the ground. When I first started thinking about this, I was only twenty-two years old, and *Dukes of Hazzard* was a hit. I'm sure Bob just saw his kid brother who'd been struggling for years and working so hard and thought, *Geez, just relax a little and enjoy it.* But I hadn't forgotten about that experience of being with those kids. I had those dark memories of Grassland I carried around with me everywhere.

When I started working with the March of Dimes, I noticed it was difficult to get new sponsors to join because the organization was specifically raising funds for spina bifida. Sometimes, people aren't moved because they can't relate to a disease if someone they know isn't affected by it. That's understandable because that's just part of human nature. People also wanted to understand exactly where the money they donated went and what it was being used for. I also thought that the money raised in a particular area should benefit the kids from that hometown or city or region.

One other thing was very important to me and that was that children receive help regardless of what their disease, injury, or illness was. I remembered those children in the hospital when I was performing, and those kids were hurting from all kinds of diseases, but all of them were battling for their lives. I thought it would be a great thing for a charity to support a multitude of causes, not just one disease, to be able to support the kids regardless of what medical enemy they were fighting. I knew all of these were idealistic values, but they were important to me. They still are.

I believe 1983 is the first telethon we did. We partnered with Primary Children's Hospital in Salt Lake; KSLTV was the first station that signed on, and Marriott International was the first corporate sponsor. Marie Osmond and her family had a relationship with them, and she landed Bill Sr. himself. But look what has grown from that tiny seed and small beginning. The first year we raised almost eight million dollars, so we knew that it struck a chord with people, and it still does.

We have a special program where local hospitals select kids to be the Children's Miracle Network Champions. For a year they become the face of CMN in their communities. They act as ambassadors and show people how important that their donations are and what an incredible difference every dollar makes. I tell you what, if you're having a rough day or a good one, please take a few minutes of your time and visit the website and read the incredible stories of the children whose lives have been saved and impacted through our work.

And again, I love the fact that we're not just fighting one particular cause; we're treating kids who have early childhood afflictions as I did with asthma, or they have broken bones or suffer from burn injuries. It doesn't matter what the disease or illness or affliction is, the goal is the same. To have that child healthy and home again and able to live a productive life. The results of our outreach, of that one little idea all those years ago is astounding. Actually, Children's Miracle Network treats one in ten children across North America every year. That's some pretty astounding figures.

People love to say that miracles happen every day, but they don't always happen on their own; they need your help; they need your prayers, and they need your sweat equity. There are thousands of children alive now because of the Children's Miracle Network. There isn't anything I've done in my life that I'm more proud of.

LET'S TALK ABOUT THAT FLAG

"On second thought, I do like to brag . . ."
— *Johnny Cash*

There's been so much controversy these last few years about the flag on The General Lee, I thought now might be a good time for us to talk about that. I understand why people don't want a flag flying over the top of official government buildings. I really do. I get that. But when the flag was covered up on the top of the diecast car from *Dukes of Hazzard,* and then TV Land dropped the series, I thought it was, for the short-term benefit for the narrow minded, intentionally confusing politics and history with entertainment. I found that to be just a little over-the-top reactionary. *Dukes of Hazzard* was then and still is a family television show about those good ol' boys from the South "never meanin' no harm." You'd hope *that* would have said it all right then and there.

I'm from a small town in New York, but I understand there are a lot of people from the South who see the flag as a symbol of fighting an oppressive system. A symbol of individual freedom. That's how I see it.

It's also like loving the old neighborhood back home if you are from Queens, or maybe it's the corn fields if you are from the Midwest. It's something that reminds you of the place where you grew up or called home. For Southerners, their neighborhood is a little larger than most. They have a deep affiliation with the land in the South. I might not have fully understood that until I moved to Louisiana. Now I know that feeling about a place, what it maybe means to someone who was born in the South and loves the land the way I love this place on the Tickfaw. If there was a flag that represented the feeling I get when I'm there, that would be something special to me in a way that it's difficult to put words to. Some people see that flag as a symbol of the place they were born and raised. That's all. It reminds them of their people in good memories and positive ways.

When I see that flag, it represents a lot of things to me. It reminds me of those amazing days on *The Dukes of Hazzard* and landing that role.

181

And, it reminds me of all those years of working at that shoeshine box on the corner or doing magic shows for hire for children's birthday parties. It makes me think of sleeping in that basement with the boiler with Mom and her saving up that fifteen hundred dollars for me to go to acting camp. Now, when I see that flag, I think about how driving the General Lee on *The Dukes,* I was able to finally see the look on mom's face when I bought her a nice car and then moved her out of that dingy apartment into a beautiful house. When I look at that flag, I see the cast of the show on that first night at the Holiday Inn in Conyers, Georgia, sitting around enjoying a spaghetti dinner together. I think of meeting Denver Pyle and Jimmie Best, who became friends for life.

Symbols represent a lot of things, but not always the things someone might assume. We need to be careful about automatically telling people how they think or feel about something when we don't even know what that is. There's a long history about the flag, and I could write all kinds of things about its history, but that's not my place or my point. My desire is to entertain people the way we did all those years ago with *Dukes of Hazzard* and that symbol for that show. That symbol said, "When you see this flag, you are about to have one dirt-road-driving, car-chasing, laughing, good time, and it won't be at someone else's expense." People love watching that opening scene on *The Dukes*, that still pulls that "Yeehaa!" feeling up inside of them and puts a shared, communal smile on their face.

The flag I know that moves me to patriotic feelings is our national flag, the Red, White, and Blue. I may not see eye-to-eye with many people in this country, but the main thing is it's *our country,* and I'm proud of it. Not agreeing has always been one of the most amazing privileges we have in America. Just because we don't agree doesn't mean we can't be friends. I don't know where the notion that we all have to agree on any single thing came from, but I promise to do everything I can to force that notion back into the pit of hell where it belongs.

I'll tell you a little story about my feelings about our flag, the flag that some people have decided to "take a knee" to:

The first time I ever saw a dead body was when I had gone to work with Grandpa Dugan at the funeral home. I was six years old, and here was this young man, only nineteen years old, who had been killed in Vietnam. He was from Katonah, New York, where Grandpa and Grandma Dugan lived, and so they had shipped him home for his funeral. He was laid out in the casket with his uniform on, and I can still see him to this day. I have never forgotten what he looked like lying there, and I've never been confused about what flag he was fighting for when he was killed in action.

I've spent years of my life singing at fundraisers for the Wounded Warriors Project and also done special events for the Forgotten Warriors of the Korean War, working to support our men and women in our armed forces every way I can for their service to this country. And like Johnny Cash sang in "That Ragged Old Flag," it may be tattered, but I like to brag. That's a different kind of feeling altogether.

LIVIN' MY LIFE MY WAY

"A loud mistake is better than a soft nothing."
— Mr. Tom King

I was on the cover of the *TV Guide* more than once, and I just want to tell some kid out there right now who has a crazy, impossible dream that you have to keep believing in yourself. Know what that one thing is that sparks your passion. No one can tell you what it is but you. People can confirm it when they see it, and they can encourage you and say, "Hey, you've got a gift for this. You need to keep doing this," but they can't give that to you. You have to find it. It's like Jack Palance said in the movie *City Slickers,* the secret is just that one thing. Just one. But that's the thing you have to discover for yourself. And for all of you reading these words, whether you're six years old or ninety-six, it doesn't matter. It's not too late for you to set some goals and decide what that dream might be for you. It may look different at twenty than it does at seventy, but it doesn't mean you can't discover something you love and go after it.

Just imagine what technology has given us. You don't have to save up for that S&H Green Stamp Super 8 camera. You can just shoot home movies with your phone. Take a trip doing something exciting, or start a club in your own city, whether it's about making movies or making new friends, there are people out there who will come alongside of you at every age to share in the things that you find interesting. One of the most important things is to not let those passions of yours die inside of you. If stargazing is your thing, get out there and look up at the sky.

But there is another important thing, and that is we have to start connecting with each other. Let's not be that person staring down at the phone all the time or texting when someone else is talking. If you want to discover and celebrate what you're passionate about and pursue those things, then listen to someone else talk about their dreams and passions. Be the kind of person who helps others pursue their goals.

Those early teachers and mentors in my life meant the world to me. I've never forgotten a single one. Those people from Camp Sunapee at the Beginners Showcase, my high school teacher, my principal, Otis, my dresser from *Grand Hotel*.

When I walked down the halls the first day of school after that summer the weight was gone and my muscles had shown up, one of the first people I went to see was my chorus teacher, Mr. King, who had cast me in the lead of *Fiddler on the Roof* in ninth grade. He didn't even recognize me until I said hello and he recognized my voice. He just stared at me a minute, and then he finally said, "Wow, John, have you ever changed!"

We've stayed in touch over the years because I've never forgotten his support and encouragement. It hasn't been that long ago that I was able to visit with him and introduce him to Alicia. He's still amazed by the transformation like it happened yesterday. He had already decided that following year in high school the big musical he wanted to do was *Annie Get Your Gun*. And he smiles to this day when he tells me that he went home and told his wife, "Well, I've found my Frank Butler." When his wife asked him who that was, he told her it was me. She very gently let him know that she agreed with him that I had a great voice, but that I just might not be the best person to play the leading man. He told her, "Well, wait till you see him. Some things have changed."

He was right. More than a few things had changed. I got the lead and was able to play Frank Butler, the leading man in *Annie Get Your Gun*, for the bicentennial year production. I no longer had that 'gut.' I didn't look like the tired, old, Jewish man as I had for the role of Tevye, but I still had my voice. And I had more than that. I had all those years of experience of acting under me. All those auditions and productions where I'd been paying close attention and preparing for my chance. I had changed to the outside world, but it was those years of acting, practicing, and not giving up that made the difference. It wasn't only because I had suddenly lost weight and joined a gym and shown up looking different on the outside.

There was another big change that year. I joined The Academy, a professional theater company in Atlanta, and began performing all the time. I was able to play in the *Wizard of Oz* and *Boys in the Band*. Mom was still working hard at IBM and holding down the fort at home, but somehow, she came to every single performance I was in. I don't just mean that she'd see the play once, *she'd see every single performance.* She wasn't a stage mom in the negative way you might associate the word. She had seen this dream begin in me at an early age, and she was there to support it every step of the way. It's no surprise that I dedicated that dance, "Smile," to her.

I'm so thankful to the principal of my high school, Victor Hansard, for recognizing all the real work that I was putting into the theater company and in school. He helped make it possible for me get the credit hours for the work I was doing that helped me graduate early.

The people who were a part of my life back in those years are still important to me to this day. I haven't forgotten their support, encouragement, or friendship. They realized I had talent, but they saw something else – that I was giving it everything I had to learn more, to get better, and to pursue this dream with every ounce of fire I had. There was never another option to me. Never a plan B. I encourage you not to spend too much time developing a plan B or C in your life. You might need to wash dishes or dig ditches while you're working on plan A, but don't forget the focus. The world has stories of people who took daring chances to cross that line where hard work meets destiny. That moment where preparation meets opportunity. But that "extra thing" is really this: being so sold out, so completely determined that you are willing to do that extra thing that no one else will do. You're willing to skip school and climb the fence to get into *Smokey and the Bandit.* You're willing to show up in character in an old truck you borrowed to land a TV role of a lifetime. I don't know what those moments are in your life, but you will. And when they show up, you have to have a crazy kind of courage to make something happen. If it doesn't work the first time, you keep at it. You just don't quit.

The song "Living My Life My Way" fit this story so well. When I first heard the words to the song, it was like someone had been following me around, and I'm thinking, *Hey, where are you?* I think a lot of people are going to grab it and use it for their personal motto. At least I'd like to think I've inspired people to hang onto who they are and their dreams in spite of the odds and everything that comes against them.

I believe the death of a dream and the death of a person are the same thing. I don't want anyone out there to have their dreams die on them. It may not unfold the way you thought it would. Maybe it hasn't turned out the way you expected, but I want to encourage you to hang on. There's a new day right around the corner. God's up to something, and you're a part of it.

This has never seemed more evident in my life than the day John Schneider Studios went through foreclosure and was auctioned off as a result. Between the financial struggles with the divorce and those two floods back to back, I was wiped out. The balloon note for the mortgage came due, and I just didn't have it. I felt like the dream I'd had since I was a little boy had died. And at fifty-eight years old I lost something I'd been dreaming about since I was eight. At that point it seemed like that dream was over. But something amazing happened. I went to the courthouse and met Paul Ferachi, who bought the property. I offered to take him out and show him everything wonderful about the land. When I did that he saw how much it meant to me. How my face lit up when I started talking about Mom being there and the work we were doing. He agreed to work with me so that I could lease it from him and work towards buying it back. (Thanks, Paul, for keeping my dream alive!) It was like one of those days that's your worse day and your best day all rolled into one. In the middle of all that heartache, we've become good friends with the Ferachi family, and Paul's son is great, too. He's very talented and done some work with us. It's one of those things where you think, "Wow, if I hadn't gone through that, I wouldn't have met these great people or had them in my life." I knew that there were reasons that I came to Louisiana and why we call it home, and that's because of more than tax credits for movie-making or for the scenery. It's because of the people.

In spite of everything I've been through, I'm so thankful. I've had such an amazing life, and I've had the privilege of acting with some of the greatest people in the business who have become my closest friends. But nothing has surprised me more than the love and support of my fans.

I can't believe now it's been forty years since my television debut on *The Dukes*. But by being Bo Duke, I've been able to be a part of your family and receive your love as my own. There isn't a part of this road where I haven't felt your presence. Your encouragement, notes, letters, and messages have gotten me through some rough times. I've had new fans who discovered my work through the different television shows, movies, or albums. One of the newest fans was a little girl who discovered me on *Dancing With the Stars* and loved every performance. I had the pleasure of meeting her and her family backstage at the Grand Ole Opry one night. She was about eight years old, and she had been meeting her daddy at the door every night when he came home from work, all dressed up in her fancy princess dress to tell him she was ready for their dance. It was precious to meet her and her mom and dad. I never take this journey for granted. Nothing is promised to us beyond this moment. This is what God has given us to experience and to share with each other. There's nothing that can replace it, and there's not a price you can put on it.

We are destined to make very loud mistakes. Credit where credit is due: Mr. King always told the choir that "A loud mistake is better than a soft nothing." I believe that with all my soul and, because of it, I have made a lot of very loud mistakes and will sure as hell make more before I'm buried in the ground… smiling. That's a part of being human. But I look forward to continuing to entertain folks for as long as God lets me draw another breath. I'll keep acting, singing, making movies, and telling stories.

One night during Bo's Extravaganza, as I listened to the sound of families having a good time and the rides going, I had this strange feeling come over me. Then it hit me. It was from those nights every year when my Grandpa Dugan and I finished marching in the Fireman's parade, where we ended up at the carnival. For a second, it felt like the good ol' days again. Like I was just a kid with my heart full of all that excitement, when the night seemed full of endless possibilities. Then I realized for the first time I'd recreated a memory – a time and place where the magic of my childhood could still be alive.

I'm looking toward the horizon with a lot of hope in my heart these days. I'm so excited about the work Alicia and I are doing, and I can't wait to see what's going to happen next. I have the craziest notion, this wild, strange, wonderful idea, that nothing, just nothing, is impossible.

Life Lesson Squirrel

- All of that hardship served to fuel my fingers as I was writing *Christmas Cars*. Not the divorce part (even though that has been spread all over

God's creation, I still view it as a personal matter) but everything else is in the movie just as it happened. A wise person once said, "When life hands you lemons… make lemonade!"

ACT V:
THAT'S A WRAP

"When you stop fighting, that's death. Tomorrow is the most important thing in life. " – John Wayne

"I have the strength of my ignorance. I am still impetuous, after all these years."
– John R. Schneider

THE LANDING: FASTER AND FARTHER (I AM NOT BO DUKE)

"You get to a certain age, where you know you can't go over the wall,
but I'll never get to the age where I can't go through it."
– Burt Reynolds

April 6, 2019

Seven a.m. and the farm is buzzing with helpers and hired hands as dark clouds gather and the forecast calls for storms. RV spaces for this year's Bo's Extravaganza sold out quickly, and cars started lining up at daybreak to get through our studio gates.

Chargers old and new, Road Runners, and Dixie Jeeps, a solid silver General Lee. Every vehicle you can imagine has been Generalized – monster trucks, motorcycles, and Ford Econoline vans. I even saw a burnt orange Boxster fixed up as the "Jenny Lee." (Okay, I'm making that up. Alicia is a *Dukes* lover too. She had an 01 painted on her Porsche to prove it.)

A guy wearing a red Western shirt pulls through driving a black '76 Trans-Am with a woman in a wedding dress riding shotgun. Snowman's eighteen-wheeler arrives complete with stagecoach mural down the side, and even the brown LeMans Enforcer "Texas Bubble Gum Machine" made famous by Buford T. Justice makes an appearance today. I was there when it all started. Both the Bandit and the General Lee. Strange to think about that sometimes.

Tom "Luke Duke" Wopat flew out, and Byron "Coy Duke" Cherry is here too, along with my castmates from *The Haves and the Have Nots.* Waylon's grandson, Whey, will be singing "Good Ol' Boys" on our Pallet Stage, I've got a set planned with my group, Hazzard Nation, and headlining is none other than Kid Rock and the Twisted Brown Trucker Band.

I've known Robert "Kid Rock" Ritchie for years. He bought a custom Bo's General Lee, and we used to cruise around Malibu, singing old songs, shooting the breeze. I was special guest at his 2018 Fish Fry, and a few months later we rode in the Leiper's Fork Christmas Parade. Bob knew about the floods and my troubles with money. "Anything I can do to help?"

he asked.

Many know Kid Rock as the Jim Beam-drinking, F-word slinging, American bad-ass, but Bob Ritchie is also a loyal friend and God-fearing man who does a lot of good things for people in need. "Can you come to Bo's Extravaganza?" I said.

"Yeah, brother," Bobby replied. "I'll be there."

I always wanted to throw my own version of Willie Nelson's Fourth of July Picnic, so a couple years back, Alicia and I started brainstorming ideas for a modern-day carnival of thrills featuring live music, stunt shows, and Ferris wheels. We figured why not have it on my birthday and invite friends, family and fans over for a two-day party in our fifty-eight-acre back yard?

The South Louisiana rains returned for another beating on our first Extravaganza, but we still had a giant crawfish boil; my buddy Kix Brooks came down to perform, and *Dukes of Hazzard* cars showed up in every make, model, and size. I'd been looking for an excuse to finally jump the General Lee, and was all set to fly, but my stunt coordinator said it was too dangerous with all the rain. We set up a bunny hop over a few Gnarly Barley kegs, and the crowd cheered, but it wasn't anything I could feel good about. My front tires hit the ground before the back wheels came off the ramp.

When the mud settled, a few thousand people had turned out, fewer than we'd hoped for, but everybody agreed it was worth doing again. We doubled down, determined to make the next Extravaganza bigger and better, but in the meantime, a few unnatural disasters hit. A lingering divorce, spiraling legal fees, excessive alimony. I went to jail in L.A. The sheriff seized the farm and put it up for auction. We were badly in need of a miracle if Bo's Extravaganza was to continue. Well, we got one.

Now we need another. *C'mon, God,* I pray, staring at the sky as the weatherman reminds me there's an eighty percent chance of storms. *Seriously? No more rain.*

Today is the day I'm scheduled to jump the General, up and over a police car while another gives chase. Jack Gill came down early to coordinate the stunt; James A. Smith built the cages, and we've spent the last few days going over the angles and distance. John Cade, who's racked up more General Lee airtime than anyone else, is here for moral support.

So is Gary Baxley, my first stunt double from back in Conyers, Georgia. Jumping a car is easy. The hard part comes when it's time to land. Good to have a few *Dukes* stuntmen on hand for guidance.

At first, we figured in a landing ramp, but Jack decided it was more trouble than it's worth. A stack of hay and old tires should be enough to catch my fall. We hope. I've waited a long time for this day, and now that it's here, I'm shaking in my boots. Of course, I'm scared. Fear is the price you pay for chasing dreams. For living life to the fullest instead of letting it pass you by.

The field between the stage and swimming pool is packed with fans, a long gully dividing the land and keeping spectators a safe distance from the stunt. If things go bad, I'll likely hit the ditch, flip, and land upside down in the water. I might drown, but at least I won't run into anybody.

I climb up and stand at the edge of my ramp. An outhouse built from junk cypress and corrugated tin waits near the tree line. Right-hand man Trent Soto hands me a compound bow and dynamite-tipped arrow. The reference isn't lost on a *Hazzard*-loving crowd. In season one's "Swamp Molly," an eighteen-year-old Bo fires a dynamite arrow, accidently blowing up the Duke family latrine with Luke's car magazines inside.

Some forty years later, I light the fuse and draw back the bowstring. The arrow finds its mark and the outhouse explodes in a cloud of splinters and red flame.

The fans whoop, and I offer a few words, introducing Jack and Gary, telling them about the significance of the jump. Seems like at least once in my life, I should slide into the world's most famous car and take flight. That way, when people ask what it's like to jump the General Lee, I won't feel like such a phony. I can tell them the truth.

With hands and hats over hearts, we honor our country as Charity Bowen sings the national anthem. Nobody takes a knee. Not in my yard. After a last glorious "home of the brave," I head up to the farmhouse to get prepared. Knee pads, elbow pads, clean underwear. Shot for courage, prayer for grace. Soon enough, it's show time.

The sun breaks from behind the clouds as I board the black helicopter. I make a dramatic entrance by riding back out to the arena on the chopper's landing skid, the *thwok-thwok-thwok* of rotors pounding my chest and swaying the treetops below. The field is a sea of orange as a legion of *Dukes* fans squeeze in for a closer look. The pilot touches down on top of the General. I step onto the car and salute the crowd with hands out, not up, then slide into the driver's seat.

A few rip-roaring passes across the muddy pasture get the people pumped up. *Dust and mud both. Welcome to Louisiana, y'all.* I jump on the E-brake, cut the wheel, and slide 180 before motoring up the road for the jump.

A practice run toward the ramp tests the engine. I circle back for another run to double-check conditions and steady my nerves. The tension grows thick as the crowd goes silent, all eyes locked on the General Lee. Some say a Crown Victoria painted orange is not a true General. There aren't many '69 Dodge Chargers left these days. Do you really want to chance destroying one to make a jump? I'm second-unit team/stunt crew today. This is not a picture car.

Jack leans in for a final word of support. "Just keep it on forty and aim for that big sweet gum tree on the other side of the field," he says. "You got this. It's time."

I head to the starting point for one last go, revving the General's horses and staring down the road at the ramp that will rocket me into the sky. A replica helmet from "Carnival of Thrills" waits on the seat beside me. Battle flag on top, number one on the side, "Bo Duke" in big letters across the back. I think back to that first night at the Conyers Holiday Inn, before we began filming. I looked at *Dukes of Hazzard* as a starting line, an opportunity to do more. *Dukes* was a wonderful opportunity. I did do more. But I never would have dreamed that four decades would pass, and I'd still be Bo Duke, still behind the wheel of this car. It's been a blessing and burden both. Isn't that the truth of life? Show me a blessing that doesn't also carry a weight.

I pull on the helmet, fasten the straps, and hook into my five-point harness. Check my gauges. Check the skies. Seventy-nine degrees and sunshine. Everybody's watching. *Guess I've really got to do this thing.*

I floor it, fishtail, and barrel down the red dirt road. My speedometer beeps at target speed, one cop car behind me in hot pursuit and another beyond the ramp. *Fifty feet to takeoff.* I grip the wheel and prepare for departure. *Twenty-five and coming fast.* The road is a blur as I struggle to find my mark. *Fifteen.* Sweet gum, check, speed – *Four, three, two* – I hit the ramp hot and launch the General into the air.

Weightless... timeless... trying to yell YEE-HAA... but the words stick like dust in my throat... a second General calls in the distance, sounding "Dixie" as I soar... over the patrol car... over the stacked tires... over the hay... *ohhhshiii....*

CRUNNNNCH!!!! Metal grinds metal as my front fender slams into the dirt. The steering wheel jerks. I wrestle it back. The gully sits left, and a muck-filled trench looms right as I fight to keep it between the ditches. I stand on the brakes and skid to a stop. When the dust settles, the General dangles precariously over the trench.

First to the car is Trent. "That was awesome!" he says. "Are you okay, dude?"

Jack Gill arrives behind him. "You all right?"

"Think so," I reply. *That hurt like hell.*

"Move around a bit," Jack suggests, reaching in to release my harness.

I flex my fingers and toes, easing my helmet off to pivot my neck.

"Forty-two," Jack says.

"Do what?"

"You left the ramp going forty-two. That's why you overshot the landing. You okay?"

Arms work. Legs work. I know where I am. John Schneider Studios. My back yard. I just jumped the General Lee on the eve of my fifty-ninth birthday.

"I feel incredible!" I tell them, pulling myself out of the window. I do a little victory shuffle back up the road, then run to the foot of the ramp and wave to the crowd, feeling like Rocky finally defeating Apollo Creed. When a kid asks me what it's like to jump the General Lee? Now I can tell them. Kind of scary, but a whole lot of fun.

As I stand with arms lifted between nine thousand rowdy fans and an orange 01 car dented in the dirt, a strange thought comes to mind: *I am not Bo Duke.*

Yes, I'm impulsive, a big kid at heart. I do not have much of a filter. I love fast cars and beautiful women. But I am John Schneider, the fourth one in my family. Knocked down but still fighting, scars and all, win or lose, rise or fall, living my life, my way. Northern born and Southern bred, a theater brat from a small New York town who just wanted to be John Wayne. And in many ways, still does. Director, singer, songwriter, filmmaker. Stunt driver. Dancer. Dreamer. First and foremost, I am an actor. The actor who brought blood, sweat, and country soul to one of the most beloved characters in television history, "Bo Duke."

The General Lee has been a part of my life since I was eighteen. It doesn't matter if it's a '69 R/T Charger from the original show or a Crown Vic painted engine-block orange and fixed up for a backyard jump. It's about a state of mind, the spirit inside, and what the car represents. Freedom, fighting the system, straightening the curves, and flattening the hills. Driving fast down a road of your own making, even if it's muddy, even if there are hazards involved, even if you're a damn Yankee playing the South's favorite son. You hit the ramp square, full speed, and keep your eyes on the other side. And if you land rough, get up. Always get up. Always keep going. Always.

"You know, John," Jack says as Alicia squeezes between us and we pose for a celebratory picture. "You're the only actor I know of that's ever jumped a car."

"Really?"

"Yeah. You're in a club of one."

We stand in the field, the people cheering, clouds threatening, but still no rain. "So, what's next?" he asks.

"You know, I think I wanna go faster. And farther." I tell him, sliding my arm around Alicia and pulling her tight. "Next year, I think I'm gonna jump again."

***

A long line of taillights snakes out of our drive and back toward the highway. Nearly ten thousand people came to our backyard party while a multitude watched online. I sang a few songs, leaned out of a flying helicopter, blew up an outhouse and jumped the General Lee.

Next, there's a movie to make and album to record. A book to write. Maybe two. There's always another mountain. But for now, I think I've earned the right to sit on the back porch and drink a slow, cold beer.

Trent builds a fire in the pit. Alicia slides beside me, and for a moment, we are still, nothing but the rhythm of antique rockers and bullfrogs rasping in the swamp. "What you got tomorrow?" she says.

"Need to get up early and do some test shots for the film."

"You've got vocals Tuesday at Sound Kitchen," she reminds me. "We'll have to decide whether to drive or fly."

A freight train rumbles over the Tickfaw. She laces her fingers between mine. In my left coat pocket, there's a diamond ring. Soon, when the time is right.

"Let's drive," I reply.

The fire crackles as night settles in. Alicia turns and looks to me, her eyes shining gold in the flame. "You did it," she says.

I nod and smile back. "We did."

As the last car pulls away from the farm, the rain begins to fall.

EPILOGUE

"Many waters cannot quench love, neither can the floods drown it."
The Bible, The Song of Solomon

"By a certain age, you know what a great woman is really worth."
– John R. Schneider

YeeHaa! Happily Ever After: Duke's Style

We were filming *Christmas Cars,* and Gary Baxley, who jumped the first General Lee, and his son Hunter who was doing a stunt for us on this film were having a conversation about a scene when Gary turned to us and asked, "When are you two getting married?"

Growing up I was a big fan of John Wayne, as you know by now, but I was also a huge fan of guys like Cary Grant and Steve McQueen. These guys were leading men because they were a certain age. At some point, maybe back during *Dukes of Hazzard* days, leading men started being very young. In most major movie releases today, they still are. Personally, I think older guys playing the leading man is a better look. You have to get that old to know what saving the woman is all about. By a certain age, you know what a great woman is really worth. I had no doubt about what this great woman was worth to me.

I said, "Hell. Well, soon." So, I turned to Alicia and asked, "Do you want to get married?" And she said, "Sure." I asked her, "Do we have someone as a pastor will do it in the eyes of God?"

We still couldn't legally get married in the state of Louisiana because the divorce was still dragging out. But getting married seemed like the most natural thing in the world. We went on talking about something else, about making the movie, and I turned to Alicia and asked her, "Did we just get engaged?"

She said, "Yeah. I think we did." And that's so funny because we did it just like we do everything else we do. We decided to get married in between making a decision on two completely different things.

We set a date for July 2, 2019, and we planned to get married right there in the barn where we'd been filming. And, yeah, it drew some conflicting opinions, but I know a thousand percent in my heart that God blessed the union, and if you had been there in the room with us during the ceremony that day, you'd have known that too.

People often remark about the kind of partnership Alicia and I have and talk about how they wish they had that special thing with someone. I mean, I've got her back, and she's got mine, but it's more than that, even. It's like we can read one another's thoughts so that when we're shooting a movie or in the studio cutting a new song, I can just look at Alicia and I know what's on her mind and what she's thinking, and she knows mine.

And if you don't think I believe in God, if anyone ever wonders about that, I can point to the day that she walked into my life and say, "Right there, that's God." I said about the flood that when you're in trouble, God sends people, and I have no doubt about it that God sent Alicia into my life, and, yeah, I wanted to honor her in that special way. I wanted us to get married. And I got sick and tired of the fact that the courts and lawyers were basically stealing something from her that she deserved. Like I've said about the divorce dragging on, anyone who knows the details of that knows that it doesn't mirror what we know as justice. That's a word we believe in, and we fight to uphold the ideal of it, but when something is broken and it's wrong, you have to figure out a way to get on with your life the best way you know how. To honor and love the people in your life who have stood by your side through all the thick and thin and ups and downs. Not just the good times when it looks like the money is rolling in and you're on Easy Street, but in the bad times when the floods come in and when you lose everything.

So, we got married in the barn right there on the property at the studio. We had about two hundred friends and family members in attendance celebrating with us. My brother, Bob, flew down to be my best man. *Inside Edition* came to cover the "non-wedding," and that was so nice to have someone cover it and respect the fact that we were celebrating our union.

Alicia was and is the most beautiful woman I'd ever seen walking down the aisle. I got choked up and had to tell myself to pull it together so we could get through the rest of the ceremony. And when I said those words, "Till death do us part," I meant them with every ounce of blood in my body.

I've made no secret about how much Alicia means to me, and when people would ask me on the set of *The Have and the Have Nots,* where I was off to in such a hurry, I'd say "I'm on my way to the airport to pick up my smile," because Alicia was flying in.

When we talked about the wedding theme and decorations, we looked around and realized we were right in the middle of filming *Christmas Cars,* had gotten engaged on the set of the movie, and chosen the day in between filming. It seemed the most natural thing in the world to get married *The Dukes of Hazzard* style.

We drove off after the ceremony in that '69 orange Dodge Charger with the big 'Just Married' sign and cans tied to the back of the car. Real traditional, you know? The only regret I have about the wedding is that my mind had been locked in this legal battle box and hadn't thought about just doing it sooner.

Alicia captured the ceremony so perfectly when she told people that it had been a perfect day of celebrating. Then she referred to the entire ceremony as being "a sanctuary of love." And I thought, *Wow!* That really is perfect. It not only captures the wedding ceremony itself and all the love that we felt in the room from our family and friends in attendance, but it perfectly captured our relationship.

On September 11... yup... that's what I said, on September 11, 2019 a Louisiana judge said the breathtaking words, "I have jurisdiction in this case, and I hereby grant this divorce."

Finally, a senseless battle that lasted longer that the "War of Northern Aggression" was over.

On September 27, 2019, we were finally able to go to the courthouse and sign the documents to have our marriage recognized officially by the state of Louisiana.

And, just so you know how the story turns out, not only did they live happily ever after... but they also changed the world while doing it.

Consider these three words:

SO CAN YOU!

ROLL CREDITS

"Use your gift to help someone else's dream and
God will send someone to help you with yours."
— John R. Schneider

In an undertaking like this it's possible to not give some people enough credit and to accidentally forget others. That's never my intention, but there's only so much this sponge of a brain can hold at any one time. For my dear friend Mike Gursey, who was fundamental to the construction and success of Children's Miracle Network. Also, Mick Shannon and Joe Lake, who tirelessly fought for what became the single largest children's charity on the planet.

To Phil Mandelker, who made no bones about wanting me in *The Dukes of Hazzard*, even though his partner in crime wanted nothing to do with me. Guy Waldron, I am eternally grateful for your imagination and perseverance. Without you, there would be no Dukes.

Brad Sizemore, you still make me smile from heaven.

To Tyler Perry, for sharing your dream with me and being a constant reminder that the only way to fail is to not try.

Paul Leim, thanks for saying, "Nashville misses and needs you." Those words changed the course of my life forever. To Bob Bullock, for your amazing ears and Cody McCarver, for always keeping it real.

Joe Mex, thank you for embracing the small crew theory and making our pictures so striking.

To Trent, Mikaela, Kendra, Cooper, Mr. Mike, Jeff, Sean, Monica, and all those who work at JSS to keep the dream alive and the place looking great. Thank you for having our back.

Brian Mayes, Nancy Brooks, Rob Kibbe, Justin Cornette, Scott Dickerson, Byron Cherry, Vicky Lanzone, Carroll Moore and Karen Bryant for their help on Hazzard history and the making of this book.

To those I have failed to mention, the story's not over. There's more to come in the next book. In many ways, I feel like this ride is just getting started.

Lastly to my smile – I am so glad you came to Atlanta! Thanks for sharing a dream with this old dog and teaching him some new tricks.

Contact John @ johnschneiderstudios.com

To support a Children's Miracle Network Hospital near you:
childrensmiraclenetworkhospitals.org

Printed in Great Britain
by Amazon

29898174R00119